STORM PROOF LOVE

Relationship-saving insights we learnt from a 1,255-people study at the time of the coronavirus

Dr Gábor Mihalec

STORM-PROOF LOVE

To Dóra

Thank you for being my partner for more than 25 years in storms and sunshine.

British Library Cataloguing in Publication Data.
A catalogue record for this book is available from the British Library.

ISBN 978-1-78665-915-6

Designed by Abigail Murphy.
Printed in India.

STORM PROOF LOVE

Dr Gábor Mihalec

STORM-PROOF LOVE

Contents

Instead of a Preface:
Performance in a Weird Shirt
– How the Research Began

t was half-past eight in the evening. Just like during the evenings of the past few weeks, I was excitedly preparing for the live event starting at nine. When I took my shirt out of the wardrobe and put it on, I saw confusion on my wife's face, as if she didn't know what to do with the unfolding situation. Then, to her growing amazement, she became more and more convinced that her husband was really serious and wanted to perform in this shirt tonight in front of tens of thousands of participants. Finally, she put into words what I had already read on her face: 'Do you really want to speak *in this* in front of so many people tonight?'

> Her husband was really serious and wanted to perform in this shirt tonight in front of tens of thousands of participants.

Why was this shirt so weird? A few years ago, I co-organised a conference with 700 attendees from sixty countries all around the world. Many of them required a visa to travel to the conference, and many of my working hours were consumed by sending invitation letters and telephone and email contacts to Hungarian embassies in different countries. Eventually, everyone arrived safely, and we had a wonderful week-long conference about family life, about the situation of women and children. After the closing event we could finally relax, having done a lot of hard work.

That's when the Ghanaian delegation came to me with a special gift. They told me how much it meant to them that I had fought for them; that after their visas were first rejected I hadn't given up, but had kept on knocking on the doors of the embassy until they finally got their visas. My perseverance and work had earned their great respect, so they accepted me as an honorary Ghanaian and gave me a Ghanaian shirt embroidered with folk motifs.

Since I was going to talk about respect in my lockdown online event

STORM-PROOF LOVE

named 'Couple Minutes' that night, I decided this shirt would be a good illustration of the subject. Respect means that I make an effort for the other person that takes me outside my comfort zone. As an expression of my respect, I even put on a piece of clothing that is completely foreign to my culture, reflecting a colour scheme different to my usual outfit and that is not even in complete harmony with my taste. Still, I make the extra gesture because I know it will evoke good feelings in others. That's all I wanted to illustrate by putting on a shirt with Ghanaian folk motifs for my presentation about respect.[1]

I thought that was the end of the story, but the next day I got an interesting message from one of the viewers of my broadcast from the previous night. The author of the message sent the video to a friend from Ghana and asked him if the motifs embroidered on the shirt had any deeper symbolic meaning. To my astonishment, he answered yes. The embroidery on my chest meant that the wearer of the shirt is resistant to strong winds. I don't know if that's really the case, but its message got stuck deep in my head. How good it would be to hand out shirts that would make their wearer resist strong winds! How good it would be to make two-person shirts that couples could put on to withstand strong winds together! How good it would be to discover the secret of storm-proof relationships and make that secret available to others.

How good it would be to discover the secret of storm-proof relationships.

Well, with this introductory story, we arrive at the topic of this book. What is the secret to storm-proof relationships? What can couples consciously do, with a premeditated intent, to make their relationship rip-proof, to withstand strong winds, so that trials will not tear them apart, but rather draw them even closer, forging their union into an even stronger alliance?

It is very difficult to find a universal answer to this question that fits all couples. Our life experiences vary, and the processing methods vary from individual to individual and pair to pair. How could any research find answers to these questions when people experience storms, difficulties, in so many different ways? How could we analyse couples who experienced something completely different from their normal life, so that we could find those who had done well and had overcome the challenges, and could understand what went wrong for those who didn't succeed? This could only really be found out if many couples had experienced the same storm at the same time: that is, if there was an unexpected situation that put everyone to the test at once, and in which it was possible to examine how people generally react to it and what really makes the difference between the two groups: the overcomers, and those who are overwhelmed. When I was planning my events in the beginning of 2020, writing down my trips and various conferences on my calendar, I had no idea that we were on the verge of such an event. More and more worrying news came from distant lands about a mysterious virus and sudden deaths. As an image illustrating the news, a bluish-greenish ball with small protruding spikes appeared more and more, and then something happened that had never happened before. The whole world was in lockdown. The coronavirus, named SARS-CoV-2, had shown us how vulnerable we are and what a tremendous effect even small things can have on our lives. Air traffic stopped, borders were closed, movement within countries was restricted, children could not go to school, and only those who really needed to went to work. Thus, a sudden change happened that put everyone to the test at the same time. The pandemic has caused unprecedented damage to individual lives, families, and societal structures. Entire industries became paralysed, fathers became suicidal, and marriages broke up. A great many families suddenly had to face the pain of losing loved ones. Anxiety, fear, and worry became the 'new normal'.

Now everyone was going through the storm at the same time, and with laser precision we could identify what makes the difference.

However, my researcher's mind also started to see an opportunity in the crisis. What could not really be grasped until that point was now becoming measurable, researchable, and testable in an instant. Now everyone was going through the storm at the same time, and with laser precision we could identify what makes the difference between couples who successfully resist strong winds and those who are eventually torn apart . . . and if we managed to gather valuable knowledge, we could also make a difference by teaching these factors to couples, using the discovered principles, to pre-equip their relationships with everything needed to successfully overcome life's difficulties. In a sentence: **we can make relationships storm-proof.**

To unravel the secret, I set out in several directions. First, I made a comprehensive analysis of what conclusions others had already reached on similar topics (this is commonly referred to as meta-analysis in scientific jargon). This is an important step, as it allows us to explore what previous research has turned up in this area and to incorporate the results into the project. I then consulted with people who have great knowledge of relationships. I asked for their opinions, asked them about their own experiences, and asked for their suggestions about what areas my research should focus on. Their suggestions were of great help in compiling the questionnaire used in the research. I would also like to express my deep gratitude here that, right in the middle of the pandemic, under terrible pressures, they took the time and effort to answer my letter and send their thoughts and suggestions from countries much more affected by the pandemic than Hungary. Just to illustrate their extreme exhaustion, I quote some thoughts from one of the first replies: 'Dear Gábor! We hope you and Dóra and your children are doing well and staying safe. We've heard about the outstanding work you've been doing with couples and families during the quarantine. We've been on Zoom meetings all day. . . . If I were not as brain-dead as I currently am, I would respond to your questions about family resilience. As soon as I get some rest I will take the time to respond coherently. . . .'

Under such pressures, these people shared their valuable insights with me to do something together for future storm-resilient

> 'As soon as I get some rest I will take the time to respond coherently. . . .'

relationships. I'm very thankful for the professional support of Dr Willie Oliver, my friend and family sociologist who, while together with his wife Elaine leading the worldwide Adventist Family Ministries, found time to answer my questions. I pay tribute to Dr David H. Olson, founder of PREPARE/ENRICH, who not only provided essential support for my doctoral research, but now also helped this research with valuable experience during the pandemic. Michele Weiner Davis, founder of Divorce Busting, a world-renowned

> **Under such pressures, these people shared their valuable insights with me to do something together for future storm-resilient relationships.**

relationship therapist, gave in-depth answers to my questions and thoroughly explored the close relationship between individual coping ability and relationship resilience. Dr Susan Johnson, founder of Emotionally Focused Therapy, also supported me in defining the areas assessed when she pointed out to me the important role that emotional accessibility plays in couples' relationships in shaping a couple's coping ability. Karen Holford, a dear friend and family therapist, not only provided valuable additions to the research, but also personally strengthened and supported me several times during the pandemic. I am very grateful to all of them for their help. It is a fantastic experience to enjoy the friendship and support of such people with a dedicated life, excellent professional performance and authenticity, whose hearts are beating for a common goal: to make the world a better place, couple by couple!

Then came the work at my desk. I compiled a questionnaire that uncovers the secrets of storm-proof relationships. Fortunately, I wasn't alone in this work either. Many great sets of questionnaires had already been created before mine, and they had rich research backgrounds, proven validity, and reliability, so I could rely on them; and there were two friends standing next to me, on whose contributions I could rely once again. Róbert Csizmadia, with whom we translated and adapted the Couple's Checkup relationship inventory into Hungarian, and who also provided indispensable help in the creation of *I Do: How to Build a Great Marriage*, immediately jumped at the opportunity and provided me with all his IT skills to find the best ways of survey and data analysis. It was also a wonderful experience to be able to work with my son, Viktor Mihalec, in data analysis. It is a great experience for a father to experience the way his son, who used to be minor and who once depended on him, has grown up and become more and more of an equal adult and co-worker. Dr Gellért Gyetvai – who was with me at college, and who later got a PhD in sociology and gained a significant amount of experience as a leader of important public research – reviewed the questionnaire, and helped to identify possible sources of error. I'd like to thank all of them again for their support, because without them this book would not have been possible!

Thank you for sharing with me with undisguised honesty your experiences and the reality of the intimate world of your relationship.

Finally, I pay tribute to the couples and individuals who completed the questionnaire, with gratitude from the bottom of my heart. Thank you for sharing with me with undisguised honesty your experiences and the reality of the intimate world of your relationship. Thank you for becoming my partners in helping others. You are true love-ambassadors who went beyond the call of duty and the comfort of your own lives in order to serve and help others.

---

[1] The titles of the presentations were taken from my book with the same title: Gábor Mihalec, *Pár-percek: Heti gondolatok a növekedéshez* (Budapest: Harmat, 2020). After the presentation I read a chapter every night for the adult audience as a kind of goodnight story. The series included more than 150 episodes, and they can be watched in Hungarian on my Facebook page: *www.facebook.com/mihalecgabor*.

Resilience, Mindfulness and Emotional Health

Every decade has its big buzzwords in the psychological and self-help literature: titles that preoccupy the readers the most, concepts that seem to be best adapted to the challenges of the zeitgeist, skills that promise the greatest possibility of success. There were times when assertiveness was the most important term on the covers of books and in the titles of training manuals; at other times the ace theme was knowledge of personality types, or the recognising and keeping of one's boundaries.

... As I see it, the big buzzwords of the 2020s are resilience, mindfulness and emotional health. In essence, they are related to each other, and each presents a different side of the set of skills that are needed to successfully overcome the storms of life. Most authors present these skills as applied to individual functioning (which is in itself a big challenge), but applying them to the co-operation of two people has only just begun here and there, and will only really reach the researchers' desks fully in the coming years. This research is intended to be an important element in this unfolding process.

The big buzzwords of the 2020s are resilience, mindfulness and emotional health.

Resilience

Are these sayings familiar? 'The palm tree grows under the load.' 'What doesn't kill you only makes you stronger.' If so, you already have an idea of what the word 'resilience' is intended to express.

It always makes me smile when an English speaker uses the word 'resilience' at a conference or seminar, and her Hungarian translator – who speaks English rather well, but is less versed in psychology – has an epic struggle over which Hungarian word to pick to translate the term properly. Even English speakers, when they try to convey the

STORM-PROOF LOVE

meaning of this expression, occasionally substitute it with another more commonly used word. I've heard 'flexibility', 'resistance', 'coping', 'elasticity', and who knows how many other words being used in trying to explain the meaning of the word. My choice of explanatory word would be 'fighting', because for me this word most closely approximates the meaning of resilience. But let's return to the original word: even if it may still be new for many, it is slowly becoming an everyday expression. The origin of the word itself can be traced back to the Latin word *resilire*, which means 'to bounce back'. In physics, it is used to describe the ability of a material to regain its original shape without breaking or tearing after suffering a strong external impact. Just think of the tensile strength of a fishing line, which is usually given in kilograms or pounds on the packaging. It tells you the weight of the fish that can be caught on that line without breaking it.

This concept was introduced in psychology in order to determine the extent to which an individual, couple, family, or organisation can cope with a crisis situation without getting hurt, divorced, or bankrupt. Paul Donders defines the concept as follows: 'Resilience is the ability to cope with surprises, changes and unexpected obstacles.'[2]

> **'Resilience is the ability to cope with surprises, changes and unexpected obstacles.'**

Discovering the importance of resilience, companies and organisations have also started to incorporate this skill into their operations. Donders highlights the oil company Shell, which consciously teaches resilience to its employees and, as a result, has a remarkably low rate of employees who go for sick leave (2%). Shell defines the concept the following way: 'The ability to bounce back flexibly from difficulties and to learn from obstacles and tense situations. It is a skill we all possess. A combination of values, beliefs, and a positive attitude that results in better individual performance and allows the prevention of unwanted and excessive stress. The degree of resilience varies from individual to individual. Everyone can improve their own level, but it always takes effort.'[3]

However, in addition to the corporate context, resilience also plays an important role in the military. The following approach was born in the US Navy Special Operations Unit (Navy SEALs): 'Difficulty can give birth to helplessness or heroism. Some become stronger through suffering. Others are overcome by it. The difference between the two is resilience. . . . Resilience is not mere survival and is much more than perseverance. It is that kind of perseverance that has a definite direction, a purpose. . . . Resilience is not born with us, just like using a compass or handling a weapon is not born with us. Resilience is an excellence that we build within ourselves. It develops in us through practice with the decisions we make and the actions we implement. After enough practice, resilience becomes part of our being.'[4]

'Difficulty can give birth to helplessness or heroism.'

The most important theme for our topic is 'relationship resilience'. I read one of the most apt definitions of this in Lynn and Philip Levy's book: 'Relationship resilience is the sum of the strengths of a relationship.'[5] The building blocks of individual resilience are listed by the authors as reconciliation with the past and emotional stability, realistic optimism, problem-solving ability, ability to capitalise, self-discipline, awareness and passion, and healthy relationships. The building blocks of couple's resilience, on the other hand, are qualities that also indicate the quality of the relationship.[6] According to the quantitative research by Sanford, Backer-Fulghum, and Carson, these include emotional support, active attitudes in action, good communication, intimacy, and shared faith.[7] Skerrett and Fergus, editors of the first truly comprehensive professional volume on couple's resilience, also add reciprocity, the 'we-consciousness' formed in the relationship, and forgiveness to the list. (I will return to these qualities later; at this point I simply wanted to list them.)

In summary, we can conclude that we are not born with resilience, but rather that it is an acquired ability, one that is learnt. Therefore, no one gets an exemption by claiming that he did not receive it as a tool given to all other humans in the standard accessory set at birth.

STORM-PROOF LOVE

We learn and practise resilience. We make decisions concerning resilience, even if we are unaware of doing so. For example, when we are travelling by train in August and there is no air conditioning on the train, and we remain calm and disciplined despite the pressure of the wailing passenger choir, we are improving our resilience. When we're doing some DIY and hit a finger with the hammer and we suddenly remember the cursing and swearing our dad let slip in a similar situation, and we bite our tongue and quietly continue the task, we train our resilience. In fact, we need difficulties. We also need storms, relationship storms, because resilience is not born without storms. Resilience is formed by the storms; this is the way it gets trained to be strong. Resilience comes to life and develops in us, not in spite of the storm, but exactly in the midst of the storm. It's like a muscle that gets strong by being worked and trained – and this often involves sweat, effort and pain.

We also need storms, relationship storms, because resilience is not born without storms.

Not only individuals, but also couples, families, and even organisations can be resilient. If the members of the relationship system come together and move towards a common goal; if they look for a solution instead of looking for a scapegoat; if they do not turn their abilities against each other during challenging times, but instead use them to serve each other – then the storm can become one of their best experiences, because it will forge them into an unquestionably solid unity. By this, of course, I am not saying that every storm is good, since a storm often can have a manifestation (illness, death, accident, and so on) that seems painful and unfair, in which there seems to be nothing good. However, even in the worst situation, we can decide that we want to get out of it well. We can't always choose what happens to us; however, we can always decide how we relate to the events that happen to us. As Viktor Frankl, who has gone through four concentration camps, puts it: 'Everything can be taken away from man, except one thing: the last remnant of human freedom to relate to one's circumstances in one way or another. And yes, you have a choice!'[8] In this book, I try to show you all the tools available to you so you can make a good choice as a couple. And let your joint choices in the storm result in a power that no future storm will be able to overcome.

Finally, among the thoughts summarising resilience, I would like to emphasise that there is a significant difference between the physical and psychological approaches to resilience. In physics, the material is examined in terms of its ability to regain its original form after an external impact. Psychologically, however, it is not a sufficient goal to be the same after the storm as we were before. In couple's therapy, I often observe that a crisis can always teach something new that the couple didn't know or didn't see that way before. That is why I always reject the following request: 'Please, help us to have the same relationship that we used to have before the crisis.' If everything once again becomes what it used to be, sooner or later they will end up in the same crisis they are in now. That's not enough for me! Once the crisis is over, let's peel off all the layers and incorporate all the lessons into how the relationship works! During the lockdown, participants of the 'Couple Minutes' programme unequivocally gave the same feedback: 'Lockdown was a longer version of our honeymoon. We got polished a lot and tuned in to each other! We still have so much to learn, but I know we are on the right track!' 'Lockdown has clearly strengthened our relationship. On the one hand, we have the same opinion about the current situation; on the other hand, we have been together a lot, and we have talked a lot. Furthermore, we had to solve new challenges together and decide more together.' Dissecting relationship resilience, we can thus conclude that we are not content with simply restoring ourselves to our original state after the storm. We also want to grow, develop, and change! As one of the basic theses of family therapy states: in a crisis, the family system is capable of exponential development. In the words of Gábor Hézser: 'An exponential

> 'Please, help us to have the same relationship that we used to have before the crisis.'

development can be observed in the life process stages of the family and the individual called natural crisis points – the birth of a child, schooling, reaching retirement age, and so on – that all lead to an exponential change.... In these instances, the family must adapt the "rules" that have so far guided their way of life to a newly developed level – it must respond to the changed life with a changed way of life.'[9] And by no means do we want to miss this progress. Therefore, the goal is not simply to survive the storm (although arguably this is also much better than having the family break up in the storm), but to emerge from the storm stronger by learning even more about each other's and our own functioning and gaining an even greater commitment for the future! If resilience is the ability to return to the original state, this improved state could be called 'resilience-plus'.

> **Therefore, the goal is not simply to survive the storm ... but to emerge from the storm stronger.**

Mindfulness

It was a hard day. The agent faces a multitude of decisions that an average person would not even encounter in his entire life. Human lives and humanity's fate depend on each tactical move. His colleagues don't always see the reason for his decisions; not everything seems logical and consistent to them. They start to worry about whether things are moving in the right direction. To make sure, they tell their superior that there is a problem and that they doubt the mental state of their team leader. Bill, the superior, invites Tony to his office and asks him some cross-questions to assess whether he made sensible decisions. At the end of the conversation, for the sake of final certainty, he asks another test question. When Tony entered the office, the screen on the wall showed a map. The question was, 'Which cities have a red sign, and where are the planes heading to on the map?' Although the question was completely unrelated to the conversation, Tony Almeida told his boss with astonishing accuracy which cities had signs on the US map; he also remembered exactly where the planes were heading to. . . . On the way out, he even told Bill how many missed calls he had on his mobile phone that lay on the table during their conversation, and who the callers were. The head of the Counter-Terrorism Unit in the series *24* thus visibly passed his test with flying colours.

I must admit, I was very impressed with this scene. I was wondering how someone could pay attention to so much at once. How can someone expand their perception so much that they absorb everything from their environment, even information that seems insignificant at a given moment, in order to be able to put the pieces of the puzzle together properly later in order to solve a complex situation? Then, with some reading, I also learnt that an average person can observe six or seven things at a time, but undercover agents can grow their perception many times over. This ability of increased awareness, the ability to absorb information in the here-and-now, is called 'mindfulness'. The concept is also often explained as a conscious presence, alert attention, or awareness. Just as we did with resilience, let's stick to the original term here as well. Not only does my multicultural and professional background encourage me to do this, but I think it's worth adding these words to our dictionary now so that we understand them when we encounter them in a different context.

However, we don't have to be an undercover agent to master mindfulness.

However, we don't have to be an undercover agent to master mindfulness. Mindfulness helps me a lot in carrying the emotional burdens that come with my job. Many people ask me, 'Gábor, how do you cope with the emotional pressure that comes with couple's therapy? Don't you take people's problems home into your own family? Doesn't all the pain and suffering you face push you down? Today I can say with certainty that they don't. But this was not always the case. I admit, I experimented for quite a long time before I found a healthy balance.

STORM-PROOF LOVE

This process began during my college years when I went to work as a nurse in a nursing home. Beyond earning money, I was also motivated to do something good for these elderly people who had worked hard their whole lives. They had contributed their fair share to society, and now, partially under my care, they could live their final years in dignity. I tried my best to tend to their needs in everything, to surround them with the greatest possible kindness and attention, to serve them. Very soon, however, I noticed that my zeal had taken me too far. Even from the third day onwards, I had intense nightmares of being chased by old people, and I was desperately trying to escape from them. Even during the day, the uncles and aunts came into my mind during studying, or even while with my family. I decided that I had to somehow detach my emotions from my work. I would follow the mandatory courtesy rules, but should not allow anything more personal. I would just go into their room, get them out of bed, wash them as if they were a piece of furniture, and then get them dressed, feed them, and go on my way. . . . However, I was already disturbed by the plan; and, when I executed it, I couldn't look into the mirror. I felt, *This is not me! I cannot treat living and feeling people as objects. Someone might be able to do this, but not me.* I finally found the middle ground between two extremes.

I was kind, but I worked with my attention instead of my emotions.

This is where mindfulness helped me. I put my emotions a little further back, sharpened my perception, and gifted my 100% presence to the elderly. I paid attention to every detail; I was kind, but I worked with my attention instead of my emotions. This also helped me to rule out anything else at that moment that didn't belong there (like the difficulty of getting my son used to kindergarten, or the next day's exam, for which I'd spend half the night studying). However, the very moment I closed the door of the nursing home behind me, I turned my full attention to the activity I was doing at the time, so the burdens of the old people's home remained there inside the nurse's room. I remained fully present in what I was doing!

When I became a relationship therapist, I used the same skill to keep the burdens in the therapy room and not to take them home to my living room or the nursery, or into the bedroom. A male member of a couple who came to my therapy, and who also went to individual therapy at the same time, remarked once, 'After a few sessions, I changed my individual therapist, and you are the reason why.' In answer to my confused question, he gave the explanation, 'Here I have experienced what it is like when someone is giving me their complete attention, and I don't want to be satisfied with less.'

Plenty of people are far away in their mind from the place where they should be. Sometimes this is quite obvious; other times it is revealed only to a persistent observer. There is, for example, the salesman you're asking something from, and it's obvious he is thinking about a completely different issue than the one you were enquiring about; then there's the bus driver who didn't notice an important sign because he was elsewhere in his mind. In the same way, there are people who always live in the past or in their hopes for the future, but in the meantime miss what is happening to them here and now. This theme is aptly articulated in a Robin Williams movie.[10] In the final scene, the divorced father is with his two children at a beach picnic. The father sits by a campfire and mutters to encourage himself, 'You'll see: everything will get better. Everything will be fine.' The teenage daughter breaks down hearing this, and says something like the following, formulating the greatest lesson in the film: 'Dad, for as long as I can remember you have been saying this, that everything would be fine one day. Couldn't it be good just here and now? Could it be that while you are looking forward to some future happiness, you are missing a perfect moment in the present? We are here by your side; we are together. Let it be good this once, here and now!'

This is spot on! If we allow ourselves not to get stuck in the past or

> 'Here I have experienced what it is like when someone is giving me their complete attention, and I don't want to be satisfied with less.'

to venture always into the future, but to focus our full attention on the here and now, we might recognise miracles in front of us. (Let there be no misunderstanding: doing this can play an important role in processing past events and formulating future plans.) I would like to incorporate this aspect of mindfulness here. I deliberately do not deal in this book with mindfulness therapeutic methods, meditations, and relaxation techniques. Let the researchers of the topic argue about these; I simply emphasise attitude, the focus of our attention, non-judgemental observance, and analysis of current events, which allow us to seize the opportunities to become good husbands and wives again and again in the here and now.

We need to move away from the individual-centred approach ... and understand what mindfulness is from a couple's angle.

After the above personal impressions, let's have a look at a more scientific approach. Dóra Perczel-Forintos, a well-known Hungarian expert on the subject, defines mindfulness as follows: 'Mindfulness – or conscious presence – is a special state of attention and consciousness that is non-judgemental and accepting, and, by focusing on the present moment, increases awareness of mental processes. This conscious presence has an important health-protective effect, because it eliminates chewing on the past and worrying about the future, reduces the risk of developing depression and anxiety problems, and improves our ability to accept the present and ourselves, our attentional capacity, and our ability to cope.'[11]

Stating this, however, we haven't yet exhausted everything we need to know about the subject. We need to move away from the individual-centred approach – just as we did with resilience – and understand what mindfulness is from a couple's angle. Hans Jellouschek, who was one of the first authors to apply mindfulness for couples, can help us a lot in this. Jellouschek lists six attitudes in which mindfulness is manifested in a relationship:[12]

- **Here and now**

  This is not the 'carpe diem' hedonistic approach professed by many. Rather, it means that the couple are fully present in a given moment, and they communicate its impression to each other. For example, there's the husband who, having arrived home from work in the evening, is still clinging onto the events of the working day in his mind and consumes his dinner without realising that his wife cooked his favourite meal to express her appreciation and love for him. How different this couple's evening would turn out if the husband were present in the here and now, if he told his wife how much he likes the meal and how much he appreciates her act of kindness and love!

- **Openness and realism**

  Couples exercising mindfulness perceive things the way they are, not painting them worse or better. If, when the wife arrives home later than usual because her bus got a flat tyre and she had to wait a long time for the transport company to send a replacement bus, the husband asks, openly and realistically, 'What happened to cause you to come home later than usual today?' – with this starting question, they can still have a pleasant evening. However, if he raises his voice and shouts at her, 'You never come home on time; you can never be punctual!' then he sets the tone for the next few hours, and it will be very difficult to bring back the pleasant atmosphere of the relationship from there.

> **Mindfulness drives us to approach the other person with care and curiosity.**

- **Curiosity**

  Mindfulness drives us to approach the other person with care and curiosity. Instead of asking plain 'How are you?' questions, we should be more specific, asking questions like, 'How did your trial go today? You prepared so much for it!' 'What is that book about that you're reading?' 'What would you like to eat today?' Questions like these make the other feel that they are important to us; and, if we pay attention to their answers, this habit will develop us into the best expert of our partner.

- **Benevolence, love**
  Openness and realism sound very sober, almost stoic, but this does not exclude us from seeing life and what is happening in it in a positive interpretative framework, both on our own side and on that of our partner. Trust that forms the foundation of all relationships encourages us to benefit our spouse, not to cause harm. In a healthy scenario, we can assume that our partner wants the best for us, is on our side, and doesn't want to harm us. This attitude helps to protect us from unnecessary conflicts and internal struggles.

- **Openness to change**
  If we treat our partner as 'guilty as charged' in a dispute, our partner is left with no other choice but to go on the defensive and maybe even counterattack. However, this preserves the current undesirable situation, because those who defend their own conduct will not change it, because by changing it they would admit that their previous conduct was wrong. Paradoxically, many couples freeze an otherwise undesirable conflict or condition because they want to improperly force the other to change. Mindfulness urges us to stay open to change and maintain an open-minded atmosphere that fosters dignity during the process of change. Not a single child in history has been scolded into being good. You can, however, love and motivate someone to be good. This is also true for adults.

> Not a single child in history has been scolded into being good. You can, however, love and motivate someone to be good. This is also true for adults.

- **Simplification**

  Mindfulness helps to 'reduce complexity', as Jellouschek puts it. It is not possible to be consciously present in the here and now while doing five things at once. Multitasking mode can be very useful at work, but it is quite harmful in a relationship if we are preparing for tomorrow's meeting and analysing yesterday's budget items during a conversation with our partner. Mindfulness helps us to avoid getting sidetracked and to focus on who and what is important here and now. For this purpose, Buddhist monks created Zen gardens, in which surfaces with tiny pebbles must be raked repeatedly every day according to a given pattern, so that, while raking, monks could exclude everything else from their mind. The same phenomenon can also be observed in a Christian context. From the sixth century onwards, so-called contemplative monks began to appear.

All authors emphasise the fact that mindfulness, like resilience, is not a capacity we are born with. It's not as if you've got, say, 7 units of it that you must manage all your life; rather, we're talking about a skill, an attitude that can be learnt, practised, and developed. No one can therefore claim exemption from this subject. Everything we need for storm-proof love is learnable!

> **We're talking about a skill, an attitude that can be learnt, practised, and developed. No one can therefore claim exemption from this subject.**

I close the subchapter on mindfulness with a Gottman quote. If you've read any other book from me, you know I keep Gottman in very high regard; in many aspects I consider him my mentor. When I was able to learn from him in person in Seattle, I was able to conduct an interview with him, and as a closing question I asked him, 'If you had to summarise the results of more than 40 years of research in a single sentence, what would be your message to Hungarian couples so they could get the most out of their relationship?' After a moment of thinking, John Gottman said, 'There's one thing they can do if they want a really good relationship. They should make it a habit of theirs that when their partner has a problem, the whole world would stop for them, and the partner would feel like having all their attention. That's my message!' What is this, if not mindfulness?

Emotional health

I was just holding an 'I do' marriage-preparation course in Prague when I received an urgent-sounding email from the president of the Trans-European Division of Seventh-day Adventists. In his letter, he informed me that a meeting would be organised two months later in Montenegro for the European leaders, and they were in great need of further training on emotional health. He shared that he had done a lot of research into the possible causes of burnout, into decreased motivation among pastors, and into the escalation of conflicts within the organisation, and also into the decrease in baptism numbers. All of his research pointed in the same direction: without emotional health, there is no development, no growth, no good work ethic or team spirit. That's how I started researching this topic, too. Two months of intense preparation ensued, and the presentation went so well that I have since held it in the United Kingdom and in the United Arab Emirates as well.

An essential part in the study of emotional health is emotional intelligence (EQ). Daniel Goleman made an attempt to formulate what EQ is, but he himself admits that it is a very difficult concept to grasp. While IQ is more about learning outcomes and academic progress, EQ is about dealing with others and ourselves; it is about practical life skills. According to him, 20% of a person's success is due to his IQ, but 80% depends on other competencies. The collective concept of these 'other competencies' is emotional intelligence. He captures the purpose of his stout volume in the following way: 'My concern is with a key set of these "other characteristics", *emotional*

> An essential part in the study of emotional health is emotional intelligence.

intelligence: abilities such as being able to motivate oneself and persist in the face of frustrations; to control impulse and delay gratification; to regulate one's moods and keep distress from swamping the ability to think; to empathise and to hope.'[13] Before you started to think how easy it is for someone who has all these, but unfortunately you are the type who does not, Goleman quickly adds: 'While there are those who argue that IQ cannot be changed much by experience or education, I will show in Part Five that the crucial emotional competencies can indeed be learnt and improved upon by children – if we bother to teach them.'[14] Thus, emotional intelligence – just like resilience and mindfulness – is a learnt skill that can be improved and developed with proper training, both in children and in adults.

Let's now move on from EQ to emotional health. The line between the two is quite microscopic. The difference really is that EQ explains the theory, and emotional health shows the practical implementation. The American Association of Psychologists puts it this way: 'Emotional health can lead to success in work, relationships and health. In the past, researchers believed that success

> **The more we progress in our emotional health, the more effective, empathetic, and accessible we become.**

made people happy. Newer research reveals that it's the other way around. Happy people are more likely to work towards goals, find the resources they need and attract others with their energy and optimism – key building blocks of success.'[15] No one is fully mature and perfect in emotional health. However, with self-knowledge, self-conscious attention, and careful evaluation and integration of external feedback, we become healthier and more mature personalities, and also healthier and more mature emotionally. Of course, this will also have a noticeable effect on our presence in the relationship. The more we progress in our emotional health, the more effective, empathetic, and accessible we become in our important human relationships. As the saying of Jesus puts it, 'Love your

STORM-PROOF LOVE

neighbour as yourself!'[16] That is, the more I am okay with myself, the more I will be able to love the other person. In the following, I present the eight characteristics of emotional health that I recognised in myself and in my counselling work with others.

1. An emotionally healthy person can resolve their grievances

We all carry pains and injuries from our past. No one can refute this. The question is, 'What we can do with them?' There is no person who has never been hurt, including myself.

I was born in Germany as a child of Hungarian parents from Vojvodina, Serbia, and I attended the first three classes of primary school in Cologne. One day my German classmates pressed a slip of paper into my hand and told me to read it because I would need it. When I unfolded the paper, I saw that the short, handwritten message contained the Lord's Prayer. I asked, puzzled, why I should read the Lord's Prayer. 'Because we decided to kill all our foreign classmates after school today. Until then, settle your affairs with God so that your soul may go to heaven,' was the answer. This was the first time I can think of when I panicked in my life. For them, it was just a silly prank, a good joke to laugh at. For me, however, at the age of nine, it was a life-threatening crisis, a life-and-death matter.

> I asked, puzzled, why I should read the Lord's Prayer. 'Because we decided to kill all our foreign classmates after school today. Until then, settle your affairs with God.'

Then – still at the age of nine – we moved back to what was then Yugoslavia. Here I experienced the next great trauma. The culture of that country had kept the vivid memory of World War 2 so much that schoolchildren were regularly taken to the cinema to watch war movies in which a single partisan hero, by himself, killed half of a German army corps. During school breaks, the boys were playing war, and I landed into the wargames straight from Germany. For the next few months, I had the 'honour' of being a German soldier captured and publicly executed by partisans on a daily basis. What's more, as an excellent student, I quickly gained recognition from teachers, which was enough to make me a target of brutal school abuse. There was a boy who particularly picked on me. On the way home from school he followed me several times, and, with his older brother and cousin restraining me, he beat me until he had to stop because of exhaustion. Many times, my face was so ugly from the beating that I was ashamed to leave my house . . . all because I came from Germany and studied well.

However, life is very interesting and full of surprises. Thirty-four years later, an opportunity occurred that helped me face my traumatic past. A boy – now a grown-up and a father himself – sent me a friend request on Facebook in the spring of 2018. As I saw his name, I relived all the pain and injustice, humiliation he had inflicted on me. Then I started thinking about what the right reaction to his initiative would be. After a few sleepless nights, I decided to confirm his friend request – but not simply in an impersonal manner, with the touch of a virtual button. I also wrote a message telling him what he had caused me in my childhood, and how I feel and think about it today as a (mostly) emotionally healthy adult person. I wrote him this:

'Dear . . . ! I was truly surprised that you sent me a friend request. If I had to rank the painful experiences of my childhood, you would occupy one of the first places. I can still recall how I entered a new community as a fourth-grader in a new country, having to leave my friends and my former life behind. As if that was not enough, for some weird reason – a reason I still cannot fathom – you marked me as your target and, on the way home, made your brother and cousin restrain me in order to beat my face blue. Unfortunately, this happened several times. Even if I was just a desperate, defenceless little boy in those days, thank God, that's not the case today. I am a strong, confident man who knows

exactly what he expects from life and achieves his goals one after the other. I stand up for the weak, and I'm able to protect myself and my family. It is this strength that urges me to face those who hurt me in the past and forgive them out of the depth of my heart. Thus, I say also to you: I forgive you! I let go of the pain of the past, because I know you have more in you than what you showed then and there. I hope that you have been able to develop this positive side of you, and that you make the lives of all those who encounter you better. It is in this spirit that I symbolically extend my hand and accept you as my Facebook friend.'

> **'I forgive you! I let go of the pain of the past, because I know you have more in you than what you showed then and there.'**

He immediately replied with a like, and then fell silent for a long time. I guess he also needed time to word his answer. Finally, a few weeks later, he sent the following message: 'Please, forgive what happened in the past. Now, looking at the past with adult eyes, I made a very big mistake. Once, if we ever will meet personally, I would like to apologise to you in person. Sincerely, . . .' As I finished reading, my pain was gone; my wounds had healed, so now I could look back in peace on this painful chapter of my past. This means that an emotionally healthy person can resolve the hurt of the past. She is not simply waiting for time to bring closure, but she takes the initiative, develops strategies, and acts. She has learnt that continuing to uphold the state of feeling hurt and offended costs much more energy than forgiving and letting go.

2. An emotionally healthy person is able to attribute meaning and purpose to his or her life

Many people think that the meaning of their lives will suddenly appear in front of them in golden letters in a moment of revelation. However, it doesn't work like this. We are the ones who give meaning to our lives, to both its small and big moments. I also had to learn this at a painful price. In the summer of 2001, I managed to get a student job at the Ford car factory in Cologne. I was very enthusiastic because, even if only for eight weeks, I was able to carry on a family tradition, as both my father and grandfather used to work in that factory before. On top of that, it was well known that car factories give the highest salaries among all the student jobs, so it was really hard to get a place in them. I signed the eight-week contract without hesitation. However, when the work began, the first shock came shortly afterwards. My task was to drive the same four bolts on the 450-470 pieces of Ford Fiesta chassis that passed over my head every day. Without thinking, deliberating or analysing, I was required simply to turn off my brain, switching to automatic robot mode to simply drive in one screw after another. After the first day, I tearfully reported my frustrating experience to my wife, Dóri. My heart clenched at the thought that this would be the way I would spend my days for the next eight weeks. Then, by the end of the first week, despair had completely overwhelmed me. 'I cannot take this any more! I give up; I can't do this!' I told myself, sometimes even loudly.

In the end, I realised that I needed to change something; otherwise I would really go nuts. Rationality and financial pressure – private university, limited earning opportunities during the school year, the promise to earn the full year's tuition plus half a year's rent in eight weeks – dictated that I should press on. I couldn't change that. But I could change my attitude.

> **Rationality and financial pressure ... dictated that I should press on. I couldn't change that. But I could change my attitude.**

I began to give meaning and purpose to this seemingly meaningless and pointless task. I began to pay attention to the label of the cars passing the assembly line over my head, which indicated to which country the car would be transported, in what colour, and with what extras. I brightened at every seventh or eighth car, as they were destined for Hungary. At those moments I imagined a young family in front of me leaving home in the morning. First the younger child gets a lift to the kindergarten, then the older one to school, and finally the parents drive to work with this car. I imagined their stressful morning, when every minute counts, when there are fierce battles for the right to use the bathroom first, and sometimes there are bargains and promises that would embarrass even a stockbroker. I saw as they struggle to get the team together around the breakfast table, and then the little one remembers, with shoes, coat, and hat on his head, that he needs to pee....

Suddenly, the tightening of the four screws ceased to be a monotonous, tedious task, but became my personal contribution to getting this family to the kindergarten, to school, and to the workplace on time. I sensed how much this family needs attention in order for their day to start successfully. I thought I had at least taken the worry of the car off their shoulders ... at least, as far as the four bolts of the chassis were concerned. Therefore, it was also up to me whether they got to their destination or not; and, if so, I would be the best screwdriver the world had ever seen ... and from that thought everything started to change. I had managed to give one of the most boring, monotonous tasks in the world a purpose and meaning: because things do not always make sense in themselves, but we endow them with meaning. This is a psychological work that increases our quality of life by magnitudes, but only emotionally healthy people are capable of doing it.

> **Suddenly, the tightening of the four screws ceased to be a monotonous, tedious task, but became my personal contribution to getting this family to the kindergarten, to school, and to the workplace on time.**

3. Emotionally healthy people are able to control their emotions

If Viktor Frankl's statement about humanity's ultimate freedom is true – that we can choose our personal attitude – then it is also true that we are not vulnerable to our emotions, but have control over them and can even regulate them. In fact, this is one of the biggest differences between humans and animals. In an animal, there is a direct relationship between the stimulus and the response. Poke a dog's head while eating (stimulus) and you will see the instant reaction. Their whole behaviour consists of a series of stimuli and reactions. But a human being is different. In humans, there is a gap between the stimulus and the reaction. According to Frankl, there is an opportunity in this gap to choose our reactions, and in our responses lies an opportunity for growth and freedom. An emotionally healthy person consciously uses the gap between stimulus and reaction. He exercises his freedom to turn the situation around to a beneficial end.

> **Here is an opportunity in this gap to choose our reactions, and in our responses lies an opportunity for growth and freedom.**

While it is acceptable for a child to complain, 'You upset me,' from an adult this sentence is an expression of his personal immaturity. A child cannot yet be expected to command a high level of emotional control, but as parents it is our job to help them develop and set a good example. However, an adult should have the ability to control emotions, because there is freedom between the stimulus (the other party's annoying behaviour) and the reaction (loss of control, like shouting). In this freedom, for example, the adult has the option of reacting completely contrary to expectations. In an angry, irritated moment, for example, she may respond kindly, with a calm voice. This works similarly to other abilities we use in life. With practice, we will get better at it. The only problem is that we have been practising unregulated forms for too long; thus, for many, negative forms of action are so deeply entrenched that they themselves believe that they can't change it anymore, or maybe they don't really want to. The little boy who learnt at kindergarten age that his aggressive actions would scare the others and that as a result he could have the best matchbox will later exhibit aggressive behaviour while driving his real car – honking, driving dangerously – and, if someone holds him up in traffic, he goes crazy and tries to push the other driver off the road, or sanctions the source of his annoyance in another improper way. He does nothing to calm his temper, but allows his anger to boil over, even though the situation might not be right. The little girl who throws herself on the floor in the toy section of the department store so that her parents will buy her the Barbie doll she wants learns that uncontrolled flooding of emotions can manipulate others, even if this will later make her relationships and family life miserable. . . .

4. An emotionally healthy person is able to express his or her emotions in an unbiased, constructive way

There is hardly any other skill that would be able to recalibrate the tone of a relationship as spectacularly and in such a short time as the art of direct and positive expression of emotions. What does direct expression of emotions mean? There are two ways to express an emotion we feel inside. There is the indirect way of emotional communication, where the person doesn't really say the name of the emotion, but simply exhibits a 'suggestive behaviour' and waits for the other party to figure out what the person wants. This kind of 'expression of emotion' (I don't even like to call it that) leaves the other party in complete uncertainty. Such behaviour drives a wedge between spouses, and, instead of mobilising each other's resources to make it easier to face a threatening situation, they cause each other additional pain that will make the issue even more unbearable. If an overwhelmed wife tells off her husband who has just arrived home by saying, 'You don't do anything at home on your own! You just sit down and wait for me to serve you,' the husband will feel compelled to defend himself. He will justify himself with a long list of examples of things that he does indeed do at home, and will attempt to demonstrate that, insofar as he can, he also contributes to the chores of their shared household. This will make the wife even more frustrated, as she did not need a list of what her husband had done, but some compassion or help with a specific task. However, she didn't make her wishes clear. The husband's attention

The husband will feel compelled to defend himself. He will justify himself with a long list of examples.

was drawn to the charges, and they practically lost each other for a while in the conversation. Everyone started defending themselves and attacking each other. How different the situation would be in the following scenario: 'I got very tired today from doing the chores. I have been working at home all day, and it was so frustrating to do it all alone. I know you have worked, too, but I felt very lonely. Would you be so kind as to quickly wash the tub and sink, and then we can have dinner and watch a movie together?' The direct expression of emotion begins with 'I' and names specific emotions (in our case, feelings of fatigue, frustration, and loneliness). If the wife specifically tells him how she feels, her husband will be able to empathise with her situation more easily and be able to express compassion for her more effectively. And, in the end, this is exactly what the wife wanted all along.

5. An emotionally healthy person is able to delay gratification

An indisputably important accessory of the life of an emotionally healthy person is the ability to make sacrifices, to tolerate, and to endure things. As biblical wisdom puts it, 'Better to be slow to anger than to be a mighty warrior, and one who controls his temper is better than one who captures a

> 'Better to be slow to anger than to be a mighty warrior, and one who controls his temper is better than one who captures a city.'

city.'[17] It is no coincidence that Christian piety values the virtue of self-control so highly, and it is no coincidence that gluttony, the uncontrolled pursuit of pleasure, has been considered a sin. The person who is accustomed to his needs being satisfied immediately will sooner or later believe that he will always be entitled to everything immediately. That's why there are so many upset drivers on the roads; that's why there are so many exploitative relationships; and – I add softly – maybe that's why there are so many obese people. During my travels in the Far East, it always strikes me how few obese people can be seen in China or Japan. Although I haven't done any deeper research into this subject, I believe one of the reasons for this may be found in the deeply rooted virtues of their culture, like patience, perseverance, and self-discipline.

It is astounding how much the ability of delayed gratification determines a person's well-being in life. Some ground-breaking research on the subject was done by Walter Mischel,[18] a professor at Columbia University who became world-famous because of the Marshmallow Test he developed.[19] In the 1960s, Mischel seated four-year-olds in an empty room and placed a marshmallow in front of them. The children were instructed that if they waited for the researcher to return to the room without eating the marshmallow, they would then receive two marshmallows. If they didn't want to wait before eating the candy, they could eat the delicacy in front of them, but they wouldn't get a second one when the researcher returned. 'Some four-year-olds were able to wait what must surely have seemed an endless fifteen to twenty minutes for the experimenter to return. To sustain themselves in their struggle they covered their eyes so they wouldn't have to stare at temptation, or rested their heads in their arms, talked to themselves, sang, played games with their hands and feet, even tried to go to sleep. These plucky pre-schoolers got the two-marshmallow reward. But others, more impulsive, grabbed the one marshmallow, almost always within seconds of the experimenter's leaving the room on his "errand".'[20]

Those who had resisted temptation at four were now, as adolescents, more socially competent: personally effective, self-assertive, and better able to cope with the frustrations of life.

But the experiment didn't stop there. Mischel followed these children into adulthood and observed whether there was a measurable difference between the two groups in the outcomes of their lives – and he found a difference . . . a big one! 'The emotional and social difference between the grab-the-marshmallow pre-schoolers and their gratification-delaying peers was dramatic. Those who had resisted temptation at four were now, as adolescents, more socially competent: personally effective, self-assertive, and better able to cope with the frustrations of life. They were less likely to go to pieces, freeze, or regress[21] under stress, or become rattled and disorganised when pressured; they embraced challenges and pursued them instead of giving up, even in the face of difficulties; they were self-reliant and confident, trustworthy, and dependable; and they took initiative and plunged into projects. And, more than a decade later, they were still able to delay gratification in pursuit of their goals.'[22]

Before you think this ability is coded at birth and someone either has it or does not, let me quickly add that it is a skill that can be learnt and developed, according to Walter Mischel (the leader of the experiment) and Daniel Goleman (the author of the fundamental work on emotional intelligence)!

6. An emotionally healthy person is able to assume good about others

A strange email with the subject line, 'Fake wife' called my attention to the published article.

A very effective measurement of a person's emotional health is what he sees first in a new situation. When he gets to know a new person, what qualities does he notice and what will he focus on? It is not about becoming exploitable and naive people who assume only good of everyone and who see only the positive in every situation. No: we all know that our world is not like that. But there is a huge difference in how a situation is assessed between an emotionally healthy person and an emotionally impaired person. A multi-page interview of me was published in a popular women's magazine. The journalist did an excellent job, but she made a mistake. The information in the 'Business Card' box at the edge of the article had not been submitted for approval. I didn't know exactly when the issue was going to be published, so I didn't pay attention to the newsstand for a fresh copy, and only a strange email with the subject line, 'Fake wife' called my attention to the published article. The author of the email is a dear friend of mine, who happens to be named Dóra, just as my wife is also called Dóra (and whose

STORM-PROOF LOVE

husband, like me, is also called Gábor – perhaps this is what caused the confusion). In her letter, Dóra informed me that her full name was published as my wife in the 'business card' section in the interview, and, in a friendly, positive, solution-oriented tone, she asked me what we should do now. She also admitted in her letter that, at first, she had been really annoyed by the mistake, but then she talked through the situation with her husband, and they had a big laugh at the end. Needless to say, such news can paralyse even the most positive person with shock in an instant!

It's a much better position to give correct information to people first ... rather than to react afterwards.

My wife and I were also upset at first, and then quickly switched to solution mode and attempted to make the best out of the situation. The poor journalist regretted the matter so much, and she really wanted to make up for her mistake. She repeatedly apologised and then published a correction in the next issue. I learnt from crisis communication that if something suspicious or scandalous happens, the person affected by the scandal must make the first move. It's a much better position to give correct information to people first in order to trigger their thinking, rather than to react afterwards to all sorts of silly theories that have already been dispersed and spread as a result of the fake news; so I wrote a post on my Facebook page with the title, 'I have a new wife! The news is fake; don't believe it!' In this, I explained in detail what had happened and made sure it got everywhere where rumours could start about me. The effect was perfect. Everyone could immediately place conflicting information in the right boxes. I managed to avert a damaging scandal which, in addition to jeopardising my professional reputation and personal credibility, could have affected another family by the false story – the other Dóra and Gábor couple – who had nothing to do with the event.

However, it was very instructive to read through the comments that people added to my post. I rarely get that many comments on a post. The number of comments was almost adequate to draw scientific conclusions. The most striking phenomenon was that emotionally balanced, healthy people commented in a positive and supportive tone: 'It is human to make mistakes.' 'No matter what the newspaper writes, we know you and know what kind of person you are.' 'They will definitely write a correction.' 'Don't worry about it; the article was very good, and we who know you also know the reality anyway – and it won't even be noticed by others.' I received a ton of positive messages. However, there were also some very negative remarks: 'You can see how corrupt and degraded the journalism profession is. They use all means to ruin someone's reputation.' 'Your success seems to bother someone and they arranged these lies to be spread about you. This is how it is done.' As I read these comments, an ever-growing feeling of compassion gripped me on behalf of those vulnerable to conspiracy theories. Then I checked who the authors of the rather pessimistic remarks were. That's when my eyes really widened. They were people who had experienced some kind of trauma or some kind of mental burden; in other words, they had challenges with their emotional health. This observation caused me to have a sudden revelation. An emotionally healthy person is able to assume good of a new situation or person and is able to see even obvious mistakes in a positive light and not as a fatal flaw. However, the emotionally unstable person assumes threat, danger, and malice everywhere, and behaves in harmony with this presupposition.

> That's when my eyes really widened. They were people who had experienced some kind of trauma or some kind of mental burden; in other words, they had challenges with their emotional health.

7. An emotionally healthy person is able to adapt to the challenges of life

Paul Watzlawick, the great psychologist, philosopher, and communications theorist, wrote a book on how to be unhappy in the 1980s that has since become a classic. In the explanatory note about the title, he wrote that the world was already drowning in positive books that are intended to improve our lives. Nobody really pays attention to these any more. Therefore, as a protest, he gathered recipes for the success of unhappiness. It really worked for him; the book became a huge success. The 'more of the same' method is prominent in this collection of recipes. To illustrate the method, he tells the following story. A drunk stumbles under a streetlight and is frantically searching for something. A policeman comes up to him and asks what he is looking for. 'My key,' comes the man's response. Now they are both searching for it. After a while, the policeman asks him if he is sure that he dropped the key right there, to which the drunk replies, 'No, not here! I dropped it over there, but it's too dark to search there.'[23]

An emotionally healthy person is flexible enough to try new methods and to look at a particular problem from different angles.

This absurd story is intended to highlight how useless it is to force a solution if it has no chance of success … yet many do this in real life. They have one or two tried methods that worked well in a given situation at some point in the past, and then over the years these became the quintessential solution, so they want to solve every problem with these methods only. Interestingly, if it doesn't work, it's applied with an even bigger force. The main rule of such a person is, 'There is only one possible, permissible, sensible, and logical solution to the problem, and if our efforts have not yielded success, it proves the point that we have not yet tried it hard enough.'[24]

This mode of thinking accords perfectly with the (unofficial) definition of madness attributed to Albert Einstein, according to which madness is the state 'when we do the same thing over and over again but expect a different result'. An emotionally healthy person is flexible enough to try new methods and to look at a particular problem from different angles. Instead of a 'panacea' used in every situation, she has a whole repertoire and can choose the solution that best suits the situation. She is able to demonstrate this flexibility in her relationships, in her work and in her spirituality. Change is not a scary monster for her, but an opportunity to make things even better. David H. Olson, a professor at the University of Minnesota, has done a great deal of research studying the relationship between flexibility and emotional attachment. He found that more resilient couples and families are fundamentally more positive about each other, and they are characterised by a healthy and respectful collaboration rather than by rigid and authoritarian discipline, and they also communicate with richer and more positive vocabulary. In a word, they are spiritually and emotionally healthier than families who are too rigid, afraid of change, chanting the slogan, 'But we have always done it this way.'

8. An emotionally healthy person knows what the focus of her life should be, and what should be marginal

One of the basic necessities of our human existence is that our lives should have meaning. As I have already shown in the second characteristic of emotionally healthy people, things do not fill themselves with meaning on their own; rather, we are the ones who, at the cost of serious spiritual work, give meaning to our activities, our relationships, and our whole existence. It was a tiring spiritual work, which took a lot of self-knowledge analysis, testing, wrestling, and self-reflection, that eventually led me to the clear statement I make today

> Humans are by nature spiritual beings ... and there is a God-shaped void in the depths of their soul.

about the meaning of my life: 'I was born to help people to reclaim their power over the fate of their relationships.' Of course, this statement has a spiritual aspect to me as a believer, because God already knew what place He intended to give me before my birth, and He gave me abilities and opportunities to fulfil this vocation. It is difficult to articulate an answer in the search for the meaning of life without spiritual road signs. As the great psychiatrist Carl Gustav Jung testified, humans are by nature spiritual beings *('naturaliter religiosa')*, and there is a God-shaped void in the depths of their soul. People try to fill this void countless times with something throughout their lives, but whatever else they try to fit into this empty space, in the end it always works like a jigsaw puzzle: only objects that fit the shape of the missing piece can be inserted into it. Only a square fits into the tetragonal hole, and only a round object fits into a circular hole. According to Jung, by the age of about 40, a spiritually healthy person is expected to get to the point where he can answer the question of the meaning of his life (as he put it: he connects with self *[selbst]* as the main archetype). So, what is the meaning of life? As Viktor Frankl put It, 'Every person has a different vocation or mission in life, so it's not worth researching the meaning of life in an abstract way. Everyone must fulfil their destiny, and that requires commitment. This mission cannot be replaced by anything else, and this life path cannot be lived by anyone other than that specific person. Everyone has unique tasks ahead of them; and, accordingly, they need to seize the unique opportunities to be able to fulfil it.'[25]

'An emotionally healthy person knows what the focus of her life should be.'

Frankl's observation is at the heart of our existence. Since humans are constantly searching for the meaning of life, if a person fails in his search, then his search will sooner or later become degraded. When he feels that he is falling short of what he could become, he lowers the bar and will settle for seeking power and/or pleasure instead of seeking meaning. I also refer to this process in the title of this characteristic: 'An emotionally healthy person knows what the focus of her life should be, and what should be marginal.' The meaning of our lives forms the centre: this will be the organising principle that defines everything else. However, if the centre becomes empty, our soul – without doing this consciously – picks up something on the edges, something marginal (such as power or pleasure) and tries to stuff it into the gaping void in the middle . . . and the result will be a distorted personality, and an upset of our emotional health. That's why we see men in their forties going crazy and risking everything they've worked for in exchange for sexual adventures: career, family, existence. That is why we see politicians for whom gaining and retaining power is more important than anything else. Some are even able to produce ideologies as to why they have the right to run people into the ground for the sake of the 'greater good'. If you want to live a purposeful and emotionally balanced life, now is the time to face yourself! Why are you in this world? What is your gift to humanity? What made this world a better place after you were born? What is the focus of your life? What is your inner driving force that organises everything else? What makes you wake up in the morning and stay awake at night? What makes your eyes really start to shine? These are tough questions, but you owe it to yourself to find the answers!

We have investigated three concepts we came across step by step, which are listed in today's psychological and self-help literature as key components of our personal, relational, and workplace success: resilience, mindfulness, and emotional health. These three concepts, from three different directions, approach the same goal

Now is the time to face yourself! Why are you in this world? What is your gift to humanity?

we want to achieve: to provide access to our internal resources and then to be present more effectively in the here and now; to be able to discern situations, to monitor our own internal state and find with compassion the best possible mutually beneficial solution. While all three concepts put the emphasis on different points, they certainly have one thing in common: they all emphasise that resilience, mindfulness, and emotional health are not standard accessories that we received at birth in finite quantities to be used throughout our lives; rather, these are a collection of qualities that we can develop by constantly learning and improving. We often need challenges and difficult situations to grow, because these bring out the resources that we didn't even know we had before. If two people in a relationship are open to grow, and want to change, and want to be a better version of themselves tomorrow than they were yesterday, these skills will improve and even multiply. This couple will be able to do much more together than they are able to do on their own. This is when one of the basic statements of family therapy is confirmed: 'The whole is qualitatively more than and different from the sum of the qualities of the parts.'[26]

[2] Paul C. Donders, *Resilience: Live Healthier, Perform Better* (expanded edition, 2018), p. 19
[3] Donders, p. 20
[4] Eric Greitence, *Resilience: Hard-won Wisdom for Living a Better Life* (Boston, New York: Houghton Mifflin Harcourt, 2015), pp. 4-9
[5] Lynn Levy and Philip Levy, *The Resilient Couple: Navigating Together Through Life* (New York: Page Publishing, 2016)
[6] Donders, p. 21
[7] Keith Sanford, Lindsey M. Backer-Fulghum, and Chelsea Carson, 'Couple Resilience Inventory: Two Dimensions of Naturally Occurring Relationship Behaviour During Stressful Life Events', in: *Psychological Assessment* 2016/28 (10), pp. 1243-1254
[8] Viktor E. Frankl, *Yes to Life: In Spite of Everything* (Boston: Beacon Press, 2020), Kindle edition
[9] Gábor Hézser, *Miért? Rendszerszemlélet és lelkigondozói gyakorlat* (Budapest: Kálvin Kiadó, 2001), p. 17
[10] *Being Human*, 1994
[11] Source: *https://semmelweis.hu/klinikai-pszichologia/tudomanyos-kutatomunka/kutatasi-teruletek/mindfulness/* (accessed: 16/7/2020)
[12] Hans Jellouschek, *Achtsamkeit in der Partnerschaft: Was dem Zusammenleben Tiefe gibt* (Freiburg: Kreuz Verlag, 2015, fifth edition), pp. 10-20
[13] Daniel Goleman, *Emotional Intelligence* (Budapest: Háttér Kiadó, 1995), p. 60
[14] Goleman, *Emotional Intelligence*, p. 61
[15] Source: *www.apa.org* (accessed: 10/09/2018)
[16] Matthew 19:19, NIV
[17] Proverbs 16:32, NET
[18] Walter Mischel, *The Marshmallow Test: Mastering Self-control* (London: Transworld Publishers, 2014)
[19] It is worth searching for the key words on YouTube. Very interesting results!
[20] Daniel Goleman: *Emotional Intelliegence* (Budapest, Háttér Kiadó), p. 127
[21] Regression means that, under pressure, someone mentally returns to a previous level of development – that is, they do not react according to their age.
[22] Goleman, p. 128
[23] Paul Watzlawick: *Anleitung zum Unglücklichsein* (München: Piper, 2005), p. 31
[24] Watzlawick: *Anleitung zum Unglücklichsein*, p. 34
[25] Viktor E. Frankl, *Yes to Life: In Spite of Everything*, p. 203
[26] This sentence originally came from Lajos Bertalanffy, one of the founders of the systemic approach, and was included in the theoretical foundations of systemic family therapy.

Stuff that Widens the Gap

No one expected it at the beginning of the year. I had planned everything at the end of the previous year; as usual, my calendar had been filled with events, lectures, conferences, training sessions, and holiday plans . . . but suddenly everything changed in a few days. Dóra and I celebrated our silver wedding anniversary in March 2020. After that we flew to Scotland on a 'honeymoon' as planned, but there we were nervously tracking flight schedules to see if we could still fly home, or if we might get stranded for a while. We were lucky to get home . . . but then the next series of shocking developments came. Everything became 'home' – home office, home-schooling, home-other-things – and after a while I felt that my home, which used to be a place of peace and recharging, had started to turn into my prison. I've always loved being together with my wife and children, but somehow the space of our home had become a little tight. There was too much of *us*, and very little of *me*. On top of that, the state of my dad gave me more and more to worry about. He had been diagnosed with colon cancer just a few months earlier. After a major surgery, chemotherapy treatment followed, and its effects peaked just as lockdown was announced. Every time I heard a national health official's call to stay home and protect the elderly, I started to worry what would happen to my father if he became infected in this weakened state. Everything piled up: isolation; increased anxiety due to threatening circumstances. Plus I had to give up on the external resources that meant so much to me: I couldn't meet my friends, I couldn't go to the gym, my congregation ceased public worship, and I couldn't recharge on weekends.

> We were lucky to get home . . . but then the next series of shocking developments came.

I'm sure you also have your own story of how these changes affected your life. No one prepared us for such a global crisis. Everybody did what their survival instincts dictated; we tried to get the best out of the changed situation, to protect ourselves and our loved ones, and to prepare for unpredictable developments. Everyone did their job. However, some succeeded better than others.

After the first shock, I also switched to survival mode and looked at what I could salvage out of this development. It soon became clear that a lot of my schedule would be cleared. The 'I Do' seminar at the end of March had to be cancelled; the training in Barcelona would be cancelled; and we would probably have to postpone the trip to Peru scheduled in May. The couple's therapy sessions had to be paused, as there was no chance for personal meetings. Since more of my time was likely to become available, I started to think about what I could do for the wider society I lived in. I didn't know about viruses, and I couldn't cure patients, but I did know about relationships; I knew things about love and its long-term cultivation that not many others knew . . . so I made it my mission to support couples until the end of the lockdown period to help them to leave this crisis with a stronger relationship. I decided that whoever I would encounter would receive enough ammunition to keep their relationship going. And I got in contact with a lot of couples.

Barely a few weeks had passed before two groups of couples started to separate sharply.

Interestingly, I worked with more couples during the lockdown than when I was able to travel freely. Couple's therapy soon moved into the online space, so I received live coverage of what couples were experiencing in the raging storm out there. Nearly a thousand couples joined my live evening check-ins, and tens of thousands watched the recordings the next day. Countless numbers of them also sent me their stories, asking questions that well reflected the state of their souls and relationships. Barely a few weeks had passed before two groups of couples started to separate sharply. On the one hand, desperate, helpless, and hopeless cries for help came from people whose financial, psychic, and relational safety net had been torn apart. They reported that their quarrels perpetuated. Due to the confinement, it was not possible to avoid each other to calm down after a big quarrel, so the next quarrel started in an already increased emotional state. Shouting, swearing, and even slapping became common in many places. Here are some first-hand reports:

'I had a hard time not being able to go to see friends or a hairdresser, or have a massage or a workout. We were just sitting at home with the baby. Sometimes we went for a walk, but the playground no longer functioned as a meeting point to socialise. My partner just came home to sleep; he was so busy, so he wasn't by my side either, so I became lonely and frustrated. I also became envious of him because he got to meet people and I didn't. My previous regeneration and recreation possibilities dropped to approximately zero because everything was closed, which further worsened my well-being.'

'My previous regeneration and recreation possibilities dropped to approximately zero ... which further worsened my well-being.'

'It was a disappointment for me that my partner worked a lot in the first two weeks; he just came out of his study to eat. I felt left alone emotionally, and drowning in my tasks: home-schooling my little son, chores, work. After a discussion, the situation improved – that is, we started sharing the chores, and time spent together improved – but the desired closeness did not occur.'

'I got tired.'

'I was in a tense, nervous, depressed mood. I hated insecurity and confinement.'

'It was like a long slope that is steeper at the end.'

'It was like when you're sitting in a miles-long traffic jam on the motorway, and you don't know why and how long you're staying there.'

'I felt that everything around me turned upside down; I was anxious and very tense due to the high degree of uncertainty in the situation. It was coupled with despair: I didn't know if I would have income from my business, if my husband would keep his job . . . I questioned everything, including our marriage.'

STORM-PROOF LOVE

'Lockdown has exacerbated our existing problems; a lot of hidden tensions have surfaced. We both bring very bad examples from our families and unconsciously copy them.'

On the other hand, however, more and more people continued on a growth trajectory. Many wrote how grateful they were that they could be together so much more, despite the obviously unfortunate things: the illness and the death around them. Many called the lockdown time a six-month summer break, and rediscovered the joy of playing together and having fun together. And in the evening, when the kids went to bed, the parents could finally embrace each other because they didn't have to get up early and leave home early in the morning. A significant proportion of couples felt their relationship was better after the lockdown than it had been before. Let me share a few quotes from these couples:

> **Many wrote how grateful they were that they could be together so much more, despite the obviously unfortunate things: the illness and the death around them.**

'At first it was surreal that this was really happening with us, and then we started to appreciate the time we had for each other that we wouldn't have had otherwise. We made the best of it.'

'Since we have three small children – two in kindergarten and one in school – I got really stressed trying to find childcare when I heard the news that schools would close. My husband and I also decided that if necessary I would stay at home with the boys so that his employment wouldn't be jeopardised, as his salary was higher. Fortunately, my workplace provided me with the opportunity to work from home from the beginning of April, so at least we didn't have to worry about finances. It was hard to reconcile work with schooling the children, caring for the little ones and running the household, but I feel that our family got stronger during lockdown. When my husband was home, he spent a lot more quality time with the kids, even though he wasn't a bad father at all before.'

'It was really good for me because I had always wanted the family to spend more time together. I had been missing my biggest child and my husband. Now I got what I had wished for.'

'At first, I felt very tense; I was afraid of the unknown, and I was very worried for my old, single mother who lives far away from us. After a couple of weeks, my adult daughters moved home, and my half-year-old grandson also came with us, so my worries lessened – instead, I happily took care of the family every day. I enjoyed the beauty of our garden and took care of the small vegetable garden. I prayed together with my family daily. So, by the end of the lockdown, I felt completely well, strengthened in faith and healthy in body.'

'It's a fantastic gift to be close to those we love. The children, my partner and I enjoyed being together.'

'Since we left our home only for work and we seldom went to the store – maybe every week or every week and a half – we barely spent any money. We talked to our friends in video chat, and with the family on the phone. My partner and I played a lot together, unlike before: jigsaws, rummy, country-city. It was really good.'

'It wasn't easy with three kids at home-school and home-office, but overall we had a wonderful time. It's a fantastic gift to be close to those we love. The children, my partner and I enjoyed being together. Thank God, we were able to relax in the garden; we got involved in many joint projects: for example, a vegetable garden, the construction of a new rock garden, and so on.'

'It was basically a good experience: we managed to set a new agenda for the family and a new rota for doing the chores.'

'I never thought we could get so close to each other (including our children), that we would become so important to each other. We both struggled not to be each other's burden, but each other's pleasure at home. Not only had we not had time for this in the usual big rush, but it hadn't even occurred to us to change this. We have been positively affected by lockdown.'

Everyone tried to adapt to the new situation. However, some managed to do this better than others. One group of couples drifted apart more and more. Many allowed themselves to be carried away by the waves, but others resisted them, took up the fight and won. It was also interesting to note in the reports that success did not come without effort. Everyone got frightened at the beginning; everyone was shaken by the new situation; and everyone had concerns. But many pulled their weight, redesigned, made agreements, and began to fill their days with new meaning. The result could be seen in the family atmosphere, in the attitude towards each other and in the quality of the relationship. And what I'm interested in is the answer to the question: 'What made the difference? What does one group know that the other doesn't? What are the attributes that are proven to make a relationship stronger in the storm?'

> **Many allowed themselves to be carried away by the waves, but others resisted them, took up the fight and won. It was also interesting to note in the reports that success did not come without effort.**

I had to research several components to unravel the secret. First, in the form of a thorough meta-analysis, I mapped out what other researchers had come up with in my study of relational resilience. What makes a relationship resilient? Which ingredients have been proven effective so far? According to previous empirical studies, what enables some couples to cope with unforeseen difficult situations, and what was it that predicted a decline of the relationship of others? I will spare you the long and tedious details of meta-analysis by only running through the most important insights.

It soon became clear that conflict management and problem solving, as well as effective communication between partners, were essential components of the process. April Masarik and her colleagues examined how partners become hostile to each other under financial pressure.[27] The research made it clear that effective communication and problem management were able to offset the effects of financial pressure. Couples who were able to effectively communicate their emotions and thoughts to each other and had effective conflict-management practices did not start to slide down the slope, despite financial pressure, while hostility among badly communicating partners and poorly problem-solving couples increased. Conger et al. concluded that, in addition to communication and conflict management, emotional availability and support are also important factors in successfully coping with high-pressure situations.[28] Interestingly, they also examined couples under financial pressure. Many studies include financial pressure as a benchmark of declining or growing relationships, and many couples in the coronavirus health emergency have been affected by financial insecurity, redundancies, and adjustments to reduced income. Therefore, I also decided to examine more closely the issue of finances to see if it had any demonstrable effect on the resilience of relationships.

Keith Sanford et al., in addition to emotional support and communication, also included other topics in their study and demonstrated their positive contribution to couples' coping ability.[29] This is how my focus was directed on intimacy and shared faith. Of course, none of them surprised me, since, as we know, the level of intimacy and tenderness is an important predictor of the permanence of a relationship, and I originally also wanted to include the important topic of faith in my research. I considered the issue of faith important not only because I myself as a believer had experienced the resource of faith countless times in my own marriage, but also because a representative study by David Olson and Peter Larson involving 25,000 couples made it clear in the scientific world that faith is indeed a very important element. Olson demonstrated that a shared faith has a positive effect on all other quality indicators of a relationship, compared to couples who believe differently or where faith has no significance in the relationship.[30] Finally, although I did not find this topic in relationship resilience research material, I included another category in my study that I observed in the first

> **Faith is indeed a very important element. Olson demonstrated that a shared faith has a positive effect on all other quality indicators of a relationship.**

weeks of lockdown as an important difference between growing and declining couples. I named it 'orderly living space and personal care'. I was greatly impressed by my visit to an addiction rehabilitation centre, where I learnt that the first step in getting rid of addictions is to create an orderly life that includes a pre-planned and functioning agenda, an orderly environment, and personal hygiene. The principle behind this – as I learnt from the head of the institution, Gábor Horváth – is the following: if something uncontrollable comes in life, it is best to start fighting it by controlling those areas of life that we are able to control; and, if we gain practice in these areas, we will also be able to face with greater power what had previously seemed uncontrollable to us. In a forthcoming chapter, I ask Gábor in detail how this should be done.

> **If something uncontrollable comes in life, it is best to start fighting it by controlling those areas of life that we are able to control.**

The meta-analysis outlined in the first step was followed by a second step, in which I had to clearly formulate the areas that I myself would examine during the lockdown, and to develop the appropriate sets of questionnaires for these areas. I had to be able to understand and assess in sufficient depth the relationship of Hungarian couples based on these different quality indicators and their reaction to the situation caused by the coronavirus. The following categories eventually crystallised as indicators of relationship resilience: communication, conflict management, emotional support, attitude towards money, intimacy, shared faith, and orderly living space and personal care. After identifying these categories, the time had come to find the questions that would most reliably map the level of experience in a person's life for each of the topics listed. I did not want to start this process from scratch, and decided to rely on a series of questionnaires that had already been used in scientific studies and whose reliability and validity had already been proved by others. If others had already created reliable measuring instruments to study a particular phenomenon, I was to include them.

To assess communication, conflict management, intimacy, and shared faith, I relied on the work of David Olson, who has already provided me with the most effective questions to assess relationships in my doctoral research.[31] With several million pairs having completed these tests, they can be considered the most used and most reliable set of questions in the world.

To map a couple's attitude towards money issues, I used a freely available series of questions from the US Financial Consumer Protection Agency, which was tested for research purposes on 15,000 people.[32]

To assess emotional accessibility and support, I relied on Sue Johnson, who created Emotionally Focused Therapy (EFT) by combining the most successful therapeutic trends of recent decades and launched an effective procedure that conquered the world by bringing significant positive change to 90% of participating couples.[33] Johnson transfers attachment theory to adulthood and extends it to intimate relationships. This means that, on the one hand, for a child to grow into a mature adult, she needs to experience secure relationships in which she can experience attachment to another person without major injury; and, on the other hand, she can be the best version of herself if she experiences an emotionally safe attachment with another person who is emotionally available to her and responds to her attachment needs. There are three important components to this emotional responsiveness: emotional accessibility (that is, 'Are you there when I need you?'); responsiveness (that is, 'Can I count on your active support when I am in trouble?'); and positive emotional engagement (that is, 'Do you value me and want to stay emotionally close to me?'). The initials of the names of the three components make the basic question of emotionally focused

> **For a child to grow into a mature adult, she needs to experience secure relationships in which she can experience attachment to another person without major injury.**

therapy: ARE . . . 'ARE you there for me?' For my research, I borrowed Susan Johnson's emotional responsiveness questionnaire.[34]

Eventually, there was one topic left for which I could not find a standardised set of questions, the one I named 'orderly living space and personal care'. I had made some interesting observations already at the beginning of the lockdown, and saw how keeping the home tidy, setting the agenda, and exercising personal hygiene was correlated with the well-being and quality of family relationships. This made me curious, and I wanted to ask about this as well, so I put together six questions to map this area. I added to these questions the usual demographic background questions in the research, and put together a questionnaire of 78 items that, after testing and refining with a few dozen people, was soon ready to be introduced to the general public.

This is much more difficult than it seems at first, as, all in all, we had to read, analyse, and interpret nearly 100,000 pieces of data.

This is where the third step came in. The questions were mixed so that it was not easy to see which question was related to which topic, thus ensuring the most honest answer possible, and then we poured it into an easy-to-use, aesthetically pleasing format that anyone could fill out online on their phone or computer in approximately 10 minutes. I asked the participants of the 'Couple Minutes' programme to fill it out, and I also sent it out to my newsletter readers and collected responses through paid Facebook advertisement. It could be filled out by anyone who came across the questionnaire without any particular control. In a few days, a total of 1,255 people filled it out; however, we didn't want to collect the data too long after the lockdown experience, in order to gain experiences that were as fresh as possible, free from distortion by the effects of society opening up.

In the fourth phase of the research, we had to interpret the data collected. This is much more difficult than it seems at first, as, all in all, we had to read, analyse, and interpret nearly 100,000 pieces of data. Róbert Csizmadia and Viktor Mihalec helped a lot in this process.

It was an incredible experience to work with my best friend and my son on something all three of us knew was going to make the lives of thousands of people better. As they both have an excellent understanding of statistical data analysis, their help was essential at this stage. With their help, we categorised the 1,255 respondents into different categories. An important consideration in the grouping was how the people themselves evaluated their relationship, and how this correlated with the results of the questionnaire where several questions scattered throughout the questionnaire also evaluated the quality of their relationship: in other words, what they say about their relationship when they know they're talking about the quality of their relationship, and what they say about it when they don't know they're talking about it. Of the 1,255 people, 634 (554 women and 80 men) were in a clearly growing relationship (both their own feelings and the 'hidden' questions confirmed this in sync). There were 317 people (279 women and 38 men) who clearly lived in a declining relationship (both their own feelings and the 'hidden' questions confirmed this). The remaining 304 people were placed in the so-called 'ambiguous' group: they felt good about their relationship, but the test results showed the opposite; or they considered their relationship declining, but according to the test results their relationship was growing. In the comparative tables presented in this book, we compare the data of the first two groups.

If lessons are embraced and put into practice in their own relationships, they can rightly expect that their relationship will face the next large storm with a bigger stockpile of resources.

Finally, I translated all the valuable insights I gained through this research into everyday language, articulating it in a way that adds to the lives of readers, so that, if lessons are embraced and put into practice in their own relationships, they can rightly expect that their relationship will face the next large storm with a bigger stockpile of resources. I am carrying out this fifth sequence by writing this book, and I will continue to do so in the years to come, when I will present the lessons of the research to more and more couples in lectures, interviews, magazine articles and weekend training sessions. I can't even begin to tell you how grateful I am for being part of this process as well!

Who fills out a relationship questionnaire?

An important question of any data collection is how to motivate people to complete the questionnaire, and how to collect a sufficient amount of data that will return reliable results. Once again, I could see for myself what a gratifying subject I had committed myself to. People have always been and will be interested in relationships. Everyone has emotional connections, and everyone wants to make the most out of them. As long as the poets write love poems, and as long as 65% of all pop songs are about love,[35] I will have something to research, and people will be open and willing to provide information about their love lives. This is also what happened in this data collection. Hundreds completed the questionnaire daily. Finally, I had to draw a line, and with 1,255 responses I closed the data collection.

Hundreds completed the questionnaire daily. Finally, I had to draw a line.

Who filled in the questionnaire? Here are some demographic background data before we list the lessons of relationship resilience, or storm-proof love.

'What is your relationship status?' was the first question. The answers: dating in separate households, 8.9% (112 people); cohabiting in a shared household, 18.1% (227 people); married, in first marriage, 65.9% (827 people); married, not in first marriage, 6.2% (78 people); and married, living separately, 0.9% (11 people).

'How many children are there in your family?' we asked the respondents further. The answers: none, 34.6% (434 people); one, 17.1% (214 people); two, 25.3% (318 people); three, 12.9% (162 people); four, 6.2% (78 people); five, 2.3% (29 people); and more than five, 1.6% (20 people).

Stuff that Widens the Gap

We were curious about how they themselves valued the quality of their relationships. 'How do you rate your relationship?' we asked. The answers were: dying, 6% (75 people); tense, 11.7% (147 people); boring, but it works, 8.7% (109 people); good, 28.5% (358 people); and happy, 45.1% (566 people). These results surprised me. Of the five relationship types listed, 73.6% of respondents indicated the two best categories (good and happy). The five relationship types were formulated based on David Olson's research, but in Olson's representative studies pairs showed quite different proportions in each type. In his comprehensive research, the two lower categories had the most couples (dying, 36%; tense, 25%), and the better categories showed the same proportions (boring, but it works ['conventional', in technical language], 16%; good ['harmonious', in technical language], 11%; and happy ['vital', in technical language], 12%).[36] There are two reasons for this significant difference. The first is that Olson did not entrust couples with the opportunity to say which category they would choose for themselves, but made the classification based on a statistical analysis of data from a 165-question test. In contrast, at this point we simply asked respondents to answer a single question based on their own judgement and feeling. However, another factor may be that a voluntary relationship test is often one that is completed by individuals who have a greater interest in developing their relationship, who read and study the topic, who are more committed to their relationship than an average person, and who engage with it more consciously: and, because of this attitude, we can expect to see this in the quality of their relationship as well. Thus, a higher proportion of test takers will have high-quality relationships than the social average.

We can expect to see this in the quality of their relationship as well. Thus, a higher proportion of test takers will have high-quality relationships than the social average.

'What is your highest level of education?' was the next

demographic background question. The answers: primary school, 0.5% (6 people); vocational school, 2.7% (34 people); A-levels, 17.8% (224 people); college or university, 74.8% (939 people); and doctorate, 4.1% (52 people).

'How do you rate your financial situation?' The answers: we have financial difficulties, 2% (25 people); we make a living from our income, but we don't have savings, 23.1% (290 people); we live financially comfortably, 68% (854 people); we can afford almost anything financially, 3.8% (48 people); I do not want to comment, 3% (38 people).

'What is your general attitude?' The answers were: very pessimistic, 0.6% (8 people); rather pessimistic, 18.4% (231 people); rather optimistic, 64.8% (813 people); very optimistic, 16.2% (203 people).

'How would you describe your faith/spirituality?' The answers: I am not a believer, 12.7% (160 people); I am a believer but do not practise any religion, 13.9% (174 people); I am a believer and follow my religion in my own way, 34.7% (436 people); I am a believer and follow my religion as prescribed by my denomination, 36.8% (462 people); I do not want to declare, 1.8% (23 people).

It has always been clear to me that women are more interested in a relationship than men.... However, the gender distribution of the respondents exceeded all my ideas – and not in a good way!

I did not find anything surprising in all these data. I had no particular preconception and didn't have any expectation. However, the following data shocked me! It has always been clear to me that women are more interested in a relationship than men. It is also commonplace that a wedding is more about women than men, and the whole wedding industry is mostly driven by the expectations of women. However, the gender distribution of the respondents exceeded all my ideas – and not in a good way!

'What is your gender?' The answers are: female, 88.4% (1,109 people); and male, 11.6% (146 people).

Where did the men disappear? Don't just joke that they are working in the mines, because I'd start to cry immediately! Why don't men show an interest in relationships and family life? When men are 'working in the mines' – that is, when they allow their full attention to be occupied by things outside the family home – they usually reassure themselves that they are ultimately doing all this for their families. But can this be simply self-deception? Can it happen that self-realisation drives us men to the point that one day we arrive home just to find that whoever we were supposed to have done everything for is no longer there, because she has felt nothing of our pampering other than material care in recent years?

It is also interesting to observe the male-female ratio among clients requesting couple's therapy. The ratio there is also about 9:1. That is, in 9 out of 10 cases it is a female who asks for an appointment for couple's therapy, and only in 1 out of 10 cases is it a man. However, when a man calls for an appointment, I know that the chances are very low that we will be able to re-establish the relationship, and we will have to work hard for the slightest success. Why? Because by that time the woman has already sent all her desperate signals to the man about the deteriorating relationship, but the man simply let them fall on the ground: but now she makes the move. It is either in the form of an ultimatum, or in the form of a divorce action, or she has already simply admitted a third party into the game.

> Can it happen that self-realisation drives us men to the point that ... whoever we were supposed to have done everything for is no longer there?

I also made an interesting observation about the analysis of a Facebook ad. I advertised a relationship lecture and indicated in the advertising criteria that anyone between the ages of 18 and 65 can view my lecture, regardless of gender. The ad text and associated image were also neutral, not specifically targeting any gender. When I looked at the proportion of men and women who clicked on my ad in my Facebook analysis, the following figure came out:

STORM-PROOF LOVE

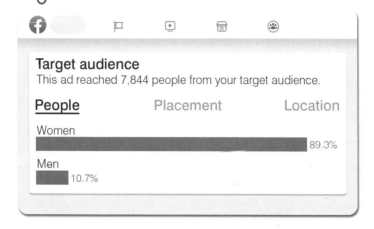

Target audience
This ad reached 7,844 people from your target audience.

People   Placement   Location

Women

89.3%

Men

10.7%

What you see here is a translated screenshot of the ad-management interface on my Facebook page. The proportion of women and men shows less than one percent difference from what our research also revealed. The topic of relationships and families is interesting to some people, 90% of whom are women! 'Where did the men disappear?' I ask again, with growing despair.

If you are reading this book and you are a man, I want you to know I am very proud of you!

If you are reading this book and you are a man, I want you to know I am very proud of you! I respect you deeply and look up to you, because you are ready to learn how you can best fill your place in your family. You don't simply entrust the fate of your family to chance, or to the more or less useful patterns learnt from your parents, but, as the real head of the family, you take control of the rudder and want to safely steer your family's ship. You are to be commended for this attitude!

If you're reading this book as a woman (and there's a 90% chance that this is the case), you're now definitely thinking about how you could get your man involved in the process that has started with you. How could you build your relationship with him into a more storm-proof, happier, and more fulfilled relationship? Unfortunately, we do not get an answer to this from our research, so I asked Imre Bedő. He has been working with men for years as the founder of the Men's Club, where he works to help men to find their place in society, in relationships, and in the family.

Do you also find that the topics of relationships and the family are of more interest to women than to men?

'It definitely appears this way at first. Whatever event we organise, be it a training event, a retreat, or even a dating event, about 80-85% of the participants are women. I thought a lot about what the reason for this could be. I don't believe that loneliness hurts any less for men. They want to connect. However, when it comes to dating, they are much more afraid of rejection, of failure, than women. They dare to take the initiative less often today, but it's not good for them to have a woman take the initiative either – especially women they don't find physically attractive, whom they don't

> **'Gentle men . . . have no idea that women are much tougher than they think, and they expect a man to stand his ground.'**

want to have to deal with in the first place. More gentle men are afraid that women will get hurt, and they don't want to hurt them. They have no idea that women are much tougher than they think, and they expect a man to stand his ground.

'On the other hand, men are also much more sensitive. And no, they are not sensitive of women's value judgement, but of other men. They are reluctant to visit marriage development forums in order to acquire relationship knowledge, because they are fearful that, by doing so, they will admit in front of the whole world that there is something wrong with them that they cannot repair. Appearing at such events, they say, is an admission of failure. Or – perhaps most importantly – what will their buddies say? This prevents many men from finding a solution, because they believe that if they go to an "organised" event about matters of relationships and dating, they will be looked down on or made fun of . . . even if it is quite possible that this is completely

unfounded. But if this runs its course in the head, the result is an inner experience of alienation and pain – which, of course, burns you, makes you sick – but, since it takes its course very slowly, we have time to be consumed by it. . . .

'And who can blame them, because many times this all happens subconsciously. They don't even know about it; they just "run the software" that "decides" it all, keeping them from regaining control of their lives. Therefore, according to surveys, Instagram is a female channel, but YouTube is a male forum. Men love to study in secret, not in public, not in front of the eyes of others. They love to read a book, watch a movie, listen to a podcast – alone, where they don't have to show their weaknesses – even if their fears are unfounded.

'It would be great if we could accept that today it is not a weakness to be less than perfect, to be at the beginning of a journey, or to search for answers.'

'It would be great if we could accept that today it is not a weakness to be less than perfect, to be at the beginning of a journey, or to search for answers, but rather to hide our heads in the sand. Today there is no other way to hold on to our relationships than to grasp all the available empirical support and knowledge that is out there. And it's good to grab these handrails together with our partner. We develop together with her. Because, in the modern urban existence, we have broken down all the barriers created by religion, culture, and tradition. So far, these have been helping. If you followed the rules, you could "trickle along" with life. But if you start drifting without all these nowadays, your life can only go in the wrong direction! You can only go downhill!

'Only awareness, the deliberate search for the path and keeping to it with an iron will, can help! You must realise that every relationship, every marriage, is like a ship sailing close to a jagged reef. And this ship needs to be steered; the reefs need to be recognised; we don't know the map, because our ship only sails through it once. All God-given means must be used if we want to command our lives as captains. Of course, we can say that in the belly of the ship we only want to shovel

the coal into the boiler, but then we should not be surprised that the woman feels solely responsible for steering, for cleanliness, for caring for the crew, and for finding ports and the final destination. Today, relationship self-development is not a 'female' path at all; rather, it is the only path, even for a man!

Where did the men disappear from relationships and families?

'In my third book, Creating Fire, *I wrote about this in detail. For the last few thousand years, one became a man by taking responsibility for one's family and community. "Starting a family" marked the acquisition of manliness, which emphasised the general rule that the family comes first. It was the essence of manliness to be a self-sacrificing man who protects the interests of his family and his wider community at the cost of his life. These two responsibilities are difficult (because you are measured on your own, and all the results are visible) and voluntary. However, in the past 100 years, with urbanisation, both have been suppressed and withered by a brand-new responsibility: the workplace. This is both easy (because you're prepared only for the job, from the moment you enter kindergarten to the minute you leave college) and mandatory (because if you don't make money, you will be poor). Men have been deliberately extracted from their families by industrialisation, to be present only in workplaces. They get out of families, because the proportion of families falling apart is around 65-70%. Those who could be at home spend so much time at work that their presence will be negligible. They have also abandoned their teaching role, so children do not encounter a male role model either at home or in schools – which leads to severe inability to connect and to form a family, both for boys and girls.*

'Meanwhile, men retain all the negative statistics of premature death, suicide, addictions, cardiovascular disease and cancer, crime, and

'It was the essence of manliness to be a self-sacrificing man who protects the interests of his family and his wider community at the cost of his life.'

other areas as well. Because a hamster wheel powered by a superhuman force makes no sense, they do not gain respect at home, their values are not inherited, and their lives are taken out of their hands. I wish they would realise that their family and their home are the only areas worth working for this much. Only by educating the next generation can we propel ourselves into infinity. Only a covenant with a woman can make the sacrifice of our lives meaningful. Thus, money is needed, but it must be ploughed into future generations at home, into values, into harmony in relationships, into health, friendship, and self-actualisation! Once again, all this can be done not at work, but only at home! Hard-earned money thrown away without action, success, and value transfer at home is money that is wasted. You must go home, because the future is built at home. And we have to go home quickly, because if we don't do this on a societal level in the next ten years, men will be left alone even by the tired women. And then everyone can live the barren life of a workplace spiced with occasional free sex.'

Can we be successful in something we show so little interest in? Why do we men expect to have a good marriage if we don't consciously act for it?

'I mentioned earlier that the school system prepares you to work exclusively between the ages of 3 and 30. Families are no longer fulfilling their function, to the extent that the family model is not inherited. By the time we get home with our children, who have been in school until four and then taken to special classes and training sessions, there is only an hour or two of daytime left to spend with them, which is for the evening routine. . . . At what point do we receive and transmit our relationship model? For our happiness, this is the biggest space that needs to be filled! Because, if we add up all the unhappiness of the world, we see that most of it does

'At what point do we receive and transmit our relationship model? For our happiness, this is the biggest space that needs to be filled!'

not arise from the workplace. More or less, we manage to navigate around that. The source of unhappiness is the failure of our private lives! These deficiencies – in the absence of any kind of role model – must be filled consciously in adulthood! There is no other way! The answer is clear!'

What do you see in the Men's Club? How can men be helped to fulfil their role as husbands and fathers again with dignity and pride?

'First, awareness of this issue needs to be widely disseminated. Millions of heads need to be pulled out of the sand. Then, from the mosaic of hundreds of values, patterns of behaviour and moral norms, a picture of a man based on eternal virtues must be rebuilt, one that can be followed in the city as well. Because, as we say, whoever has a picture in his head of what kind of person (man, husband, and so on) he wants to be, that he is able to become! The man who has no image of this kind in his head is unable to transform himself into this image.

> **'Moreover, in modern culture, masculinity alone is considered toxic, infectiously toxic!'**

And this image exists today not because it has been worn away throughout the generations, but because it is being deliberately destroyed by the mainstream media. Today, violence, expropriation, rigidity, stubbornness, laziness, irresponsibility, and other things are all attributed to men. Moreover, in modern culture, masculinity alone is considered toxic, infectiously toxic! It is hard to take all this in! So we need to rebuild the image of the man we should become if we want a woman to look up to us and to stand by us, if we want self-esteem, if we want to feel that our existence fills a gap that can be filled only by us, and if we want to understand that our sacrifice is an indispensable stone in the road of the future! This is what I am building in my books Male Energy, Trustworthy Man *and* Creative Fire, *through my TV show, my presentations, the nearly 160,000-strong Facebook community with the million-visitor website, the Granite Lion Male Role Model*

STORM-PROOF LOVE

Award, the Tree of Male Responsibility, Culture from Father, Shoulder to Shoulder with Dad, the Couple's Party, the Men's Club Picnic, Father-Son and Father-Daughter camps, and many other social motivation projects we have launched. Because, in addition to problem awareness and visioning, we need to give strength and motivation, to create a desire in millions of people to start taking action as a man at home, on their own, just to make their own lives successful! Imagine such men – by the side of a woman, lovingly guiding their children! Because our world will not be similar to the technologies we develop, to the kind of economy or the infrastructure we build, but to the kind of children we raise! If we raise good adults out of our children, they will build good technology, a good economy, and good infrastructure! Then we will be satisfied, healthy, cheerful old people!'

> **'Imagine such men – by the side of a woman, lovingly guiding their children!'**

What advice would you give to a woman who is so eager to improve her relationship, who wants to learn and change, but her husband isn't up to it? Can the relationship change in the right direction if only the woman acts?

'I think the women can only convince a man to follow with creativity. If a woman is forceful, it won't work much. Women's leadership is about creating demand. You must start guiding the man when he responds to the "I want someone to bring me a star" wishes that are sighed and not shouted . . . because then he will feel that he can be someone and will jump to meet your request. When there's been trouble for a while, when the man doesn't jump to meet the woman's needs, then comes the other creative solution – to arouse his interest. A man does a lot to maintain the external image of himself, to preserve his role in the hierarchy, to regain his ability to act, and so on. The motivation to keep the family should be linked to this as well. And we should dig even deeper at this point. I have an hour-and-a-half lecture on what a woman can do as a mother and wife in the formation of a man. The ideological approach and techniques listed there, but which cannot be explained in depth, can

also help. It's not easy for our women, but I wish they wouldn't give up. To those who are already engaged in this task I should relay the wisdom of Matthew's gospel: "Be as shrewd as snakes and as innocent as doves" (Matthew 10:16, NIV); and, I shall add, they should be also persistent. Whoever is at the life stage of choosing a partner, choose ruthlessly well! I know it's kind of a strange pair of words, but please try it out!'

---

[27] April S. Masarik, Monika J. Martin, Emilio Ferrer, Frederick O. Lorenz, Katherine J. Conger, Rand D. Conger, 'Couple Resilience to Economic Pressure Over Time and Across Generations', in: *Journal of Marriage and Family*, 2016/78 (2), pp. 326-345

[28] R. D. Conger, M. A. Rueter, G. H. Elder Jr.: 'Couple Resilience to Economic Pressure', in: *Journal of Personality and Social Psychology*, 1999/76 (1), pp. 54-71

[29] Sanford et al., 'Couple Resilience Inventory: Two Dimensions of Naturally Occurring Relationship Behaviour During Stressful Life Events', in: *Psychological Assessment*, 2016/28 (10), pp. 1243-1254

[30] Peter J. Larson and David H. Olson, 'Spiritual Beliefs and Marriage: A National Survey Based on ENRICH', source: *https://prepare-enrich.com/pe_main_site_content/pdf/research/beliefsandmarriage.pdf* (accessed: 4/8/2020)

[31] Mihalec Gábor, *A lelkigondozás és a pszichoterápia határkérdései a házasságggondozásban* (Budapest: Károli Gáspár Református Egyetem, 2013), pp. 323-326, source: *http://corvina.kre.hu:8080/phd/Mihalec_Gabor_Disszertacio.pdf* (accessed: 4/8/2020)

[32] *Measuring Financial Well-being: A Guide to Using the CFPB Financial Well-being Scale* (Consumer Financial Protection Bureau, 2015), source: *https://files.consumerfinance.gov/f/201512_cfpb_financial-well-being-user-guide-scale.pdf* (accessed: 4/8/2020)

[33] Susan M. Johnson, *The Practice of Emotionally Focused Couple Therapy: Creating Connection* (London, New York: Routledge, 2004), Kindle edition

[34] Sue Johnson, *Hold Me Tight! Seven Conversations for a Lifetime of Love* (New York, Boston, London: Little, Brown and Company, 2008), Kindle edition

[35] Chad Swiatowicz discovered an interesting result in his research at the University of Florida. From the '60s, he examined the subject of popular songs and found that love dominated in most of them. He predicts that the proportion of love songs in the pop market will grow by 10% every 34 years. While between 1968 and 1971 50% of the songs were about love, between 2002 and 2005 that number was already 60%. We are currently at 65%. Source: *https://news.ufl.edu/archive/2007/05/love-still-dominates-pop-song-lyrics-but-with-raunchier-language.html* (accessed: 5/8/2020).

[36] David H. Olson, *Handbuch für Berater: PREPARE/ ENRICH* (Minneapolis: Life INNOVATIONS, 2000), p. 77

STORM-PROOF LOVE

The Impact of Lockdown on Relationships

The lockdown revealed the size of our reserves. You will read this sentence from me several times in the book, because it became one of the most important conclusions that I drew. The level of storm-resistance of a relationship is not determined by the storm, but by our actions and attitudes before the storm. Thus, families who experienced escalating conflicts during lockdown did not become unusually quarrelsome during the lockdown itself. They had failed to develop good conflict-management skills before the lockdown period, but the lower demands of daily life had not confronted them with their shortcomings. Similarly, families who found themselves in a financially difficult situation during lockdown did not become impoverished during the lockdown. They hadn't had enough financial reserves before lockdown, potentially allowing themselves to end up in a debt trap. They were able to pull through from one month to the next without the system collapsing during storm-free weather, but the lockdown showed how vulnerable they were. Lockdown has shown how many reserves we had financially, emotionally, mentally, and even in terms of our health. One proverb states, 'Opportunity makes a thief.' However, I do not agree with this proverb. The opportunity – in our case, the emergency caused by the coronavirus – only shed light on what had been there always, only it hadn't been visible. The person who was kind before the crisis could maintain his or her kindness, but the person who had already had temper problems before simply became worse and more abusive. Those who managed their money responsibly and consciously before had reserves to tap into, but those who relied on advertisements and became indebted got into a very difficult situation during lockdown.

> The person who was kind before the crisis could maintain his or her kindness, but the person who had already had temper problems before simply became worse and more abusive.

The Impact of Lockdown on Relationships

Let's have a look at the summaries about life during lockdown and its effects on relationships!

First, let's have a look at the proportion of respondents who spent the first wave of the pandemic at home. 'During the pandemic, we spent most of our time at home, locked in' – 46.4% of respondents (582 people) fully agreed, 21.3% (267 people) somewhat agreed, and the remaining 32.3% (406 people) were in the undecided, somewhat disagreeing, and not agreeing at all categories. As the numbers show, the majority of respondents (67.7%, 849 people) changed their lives significantly during lockdown; they obeyed the 'stay at home!' campaign, and settled into working from home. However, this also changed their relationship dynamics.

'Lockdown has strengthened our relationship,' was the next statement, to which the following responses came. The majority of subjects in the study (60.4%, 758 people) felt that their relationship had strengthened during lockdown. However, almost a fifth (19.8%, 249 people) experienced a decline in their relationship. As we broadened the focus from the couple to the family, we articulated the following line: 'During the pandemic, we grew closer to each other as a family.' With the help of this sentence, we mapped out the changes. According to the answers, 70.9% of families (889 people) were brought closer together by the lockdown, while 16.9% (212 people) moved further away from each other. The exact reasons for this will be examined in detail in the next chapter, which is also the most important part of the book. It will become clear in that chapter what those who developed did well during the lockdown, and where those who failed started to decline in their relationship.

> Lockdown could have two possible outcomes for any relationship. Either couples would divorce en masse, or there would be a baby boom nine months later.

The press joked a lot that lockdown could have two possible outcomes for any relationship. Either couples would divorce en masse, or there would be a baby boom nine months later. Let's look at how the confinement affected the intimate lives of the couples: 'The confinement improved our intimacy.' According to the responses, half of the respondents (49.3%, 618 people) had a boom in their intimacy.

However, less positive developments also occurred during confinement, which were also covered extensively in the news. During lockdown, the financial stability of many families got into jeopardy. Factories shut down; entire economic sectors went nearly bankrupt; companies became insolvent and started to lay off their employees. In the case of our respondents, the result was deduced from the answers given to the question, 'Due to the pandemic, our revenues have dropped significantly.' Positively, 22.1% of respondents (277 people) somewhat disagreed, and 46.7% (586 people) fully disagreed with this statement. The remaining 31.2% (392 people) were divided between the undecided, somewhat agreeing, and fully agreeing categories.

The French government has set aside 20,000 hotel rooms to be safe places for abused wives and children during the lockdown.

It has also been shared frequently that abuse has taken place in many families. Anyone who had previously had a tendency to violence before had stepped up their aggression. Anyone who 'just' used to shout that far had started slapping; the ones who had so far 'only' slapped others had started strangling.... The French government has set aside 20,000 hotel rooms to be safe places for abused wives and children during the lockdown. Similar measures could be seen in other countries as well. Helplines were busy, and counsellors had to deal with increased interest and enquiries. The trouble was compounded by the fact that, because of having been confined to their homes themselves, members of the social signalling system (teachers, nurses, pastors, GPs, neighbours, and so on) could not even monitor the lives of families to prevent tragedies. I will return to this issue in detail in the chapter about conflict management; for now, let's just have a look at the numbers. 'During the pandemic, my partner was verbally or physically harsh' was the statement we asked people to respond to.

The Impact of Lockdown on Relationships

As has already been shown in the responses to previous statements, the majority of the respondents were individuals in a good relationship with a balanced background, but even among them there have been verbal and/or physical excesses. More than two thirds of those surveyed (72.5%, 910 people) answered with a definite no, while the others (albeit scattered) gave an answer (from a definite yes to a hesitant no) that indicated abusive behaviour to some degree. My personal experience with other tests has convinced me that the topic of abuse is so imbued with fear and shame that, even with an anonymous questionnaire, respondents are inclined to make their situation look better than it really is. If someone admits that their partner sometimes gives them a little smack, then we can safely assume that slapping is regular occurrence, and even more brutal things happen. This is very sad, as 27.5% of the respondents (345 people) suffered some form of abuse during lockdown. And that is exactly 27.5% more than it should be! Let's have a look at the other side as well, although we treat the data with caution again, as shame affects these results as well, and we also have a strong tendency to beautify our own negative behaviour. 'The lockdown brought out in me that I was verbally or physically harsh with my partner' was the reverse statement. This time 8.5% (106 people) agreed, while 66.8% (838 people) disagreed fully, 19.8% (249 people) somewhat disagreed, and 4.9% (62 people) could not decide what to say.

In addition to data on abuse, I was also interested in how alcohol consumption changed during the pandemic. I know from the stories of many couples that periods of abuse are often associated with increased drinking by the abuser. Of course, we also treat this data with reservation, because, similarly to abuse, people like to improve their appearances because of shame. 'I drank more alcohol during the

This is very sad, as 27.5% of the respondents (345 people) suffered some form of abuse during lockdown. And that is exactly 27.5% more than it should be!

lockdown than usual' – 3.5% of respondents (44 people) said a definite yes; 7.5% (94 people) strongly agreed; 75.7% (950 people) disagreed; 9.4% (118 people) somewhat disagreed; and 3.9% (49 people) could not decide.

It is impossible not to realise how the answers to the last three questions are in sync. Although there are minimal differences, all three show the same trend in their order of magnitude. We may add to these trajectories the natural consequence of negative processes: namely, how many people thought seriously about divorce during lockdown. 'During the lockdown, I seriously thought about the idea of divorce,' asked the questionnaire: 5.5% (69 people) fully agreed; the same number (5.5%, 69 people) somewhat agreed; 76.2% (956 people) strongly disagreed; 9.7% (122 people) somewhat disagreed; and 3.1% (39 people) could not decide.

Compared to the previous questions, we see only minimal quantitative differences here as well. According to these, violence, alcohol, and divorce are automatic responses of many people to a crisis beyond their power. Just like characters in movies, when they come under pressure, they also reach for a glass of whisky. I know this sounds a little harsh, and obviously we can't generalise it, but the numbers above suggest that, while most respondents had enough reserves (emotionally, financially, relationally, and so on) to face the challenges of the pandemic, those who had exhausted their reserves more easily reached for the listed – obviously flawed – 'solutions'.

This is the most exciting part of the whole research!

After the first rather superficial comparison, let's delve into the details. The time has come to examine the components of relationship resilience already defined above, and to see how respondents who emerged from lockdown with a strengthened relationship differed from those whose relationship started to decline. This is the most exciting part of the whole research!

The Storm Brings
Our Reserves to the Surface

Relationship Resilience on the Balance Sheet

For a long time, biology lessons based on the theory of evolution have taught that the 'fittest' always survive. Though sometimes understood as meaning that the most physically fit survive, it is actually intended to mean that those who are best fitted to their environment survive: those with the most advantageous adaptations. The skill of adapting to one's circumstances is surely very valuable for the survival of human relationships too. The key to survival, or to storm resistance, is the ability to adapt to changed circumstances. Of course, adaptation is greatly enhanced if we have not only one solution scheme that we apply to each situation, or rather force onto it, but rather a wide repertoire of solutions from which we can pick and choose the one that best suits the

> The key to survival, or to storm resistance, is the ability to adapt to changed circumstances.

challenges of the given situation. In fact, one of the biggest barriers to development, as I have already explained in the chapter on emotional health, is the insistence on clinging to old patterns to the degree of resisting new solutions. Many families and work, religious, sport, and other communities have fallen apart because of the phrase, 'But this is how we've ALWAYS done it!'

In the following, I present the differences identified by our research into growing and declining relationships in seven areas that determine relationship resilience (communication, conflict management, financial resources, intimacy, emotional reach, orderly living space, and spirituality); and, based on the results, I will present a range of possibilities to show what you can do with your partner to increase the resilience of your relationship. I believe this is the most important part of the whole book.

STORM-PROOF LOVE

Communication
– the Alpha and Omega of Storm-proof Love

My train was already halfway to its destination when a new passenger boarded the intercity train between Szeged and Budapest and took a seat just behind unlucky me. The man, who was my age, spoke at length on the phone with a woman, presumably with his partner. The conversation took place in a very heated, emotional manner, in which the man sometimes raised his voice and shouted, and at other times he barely whispered with a silent, crying voice. They felt they were in trouble. My therapist's ears couldn't ignore the dialogue; and, as I listened to them, I noticed that even my stomach was also signalling tension more and more strongly. During a therapy session, I handle the tensions quite well because I have the opportunity to intervene, and in addition I also have the mandate of the couple to intervene, as they came to me to help them to do things differently. In that situation, however, I had neither the opportunity nor the mandate, only my forced exposure to the negative atmosphere generated by the man. Sure, I could have addressed him, but publicly confronting an emotionally uncontrolled person doesn't always pay off . . . so I resolved to spend my time usefully and observe where this man failed in his conversation. During the conversation, he used the words f*** and b**** remarkably frequently, which I never use, nor did I allow my children to use. In addition, I heard many instances when he cut off the woman's words and tried to overpower her with sheer volume. I also observed his use of personal pronouns, and noticed that he used the word 'you' for most of the conversation, and very rarely used 'I', and never used 'we'. As for the content of the conversation, I noticed that he often tried to suppress the other with power and authority, but showed no sign that he understood or even heard what the other party had just said. He didn't even give his listener a glimpse (or should I say his 'listeners', as after a while the whole carriage became part of his quarrel) of how he got from one conclusion to another, what processes were going on in him. He also seemed to avoid emotions, as if they were something horrifying to him. In short, the conversation was a disaster! If I had wanted to make every possible mistake, I would have done exactly what this man did. However, I did not share this story in order to win you over as my ally in judging this man. I don't want to judge; I want to learn. An important lesson was how much I had been affected by the prolonged scene in which I had become unwillingly involved. I was reminded of a scene from the movie *Grown Ups*. In the comedy, some childhood friends travel with their family for a weekend get-together in a small rural town that once meant the whole world to them. They also

In retrospect I am very grateful for boarding that train that day. It turned out to be a big lesson for me.

visit the local swimming pool to show their children where they used to paddle a long time ago. One of them remembers that in the pool they were always told that a special chemical had been poured into the water, and if someone would pee, the water would discolour around that person. One of the brainy men came up with the idea to test the truth of that claim. They carry out the experiment, and what a surprise: the water around them did turn dark blue, and everyone ran out of the pool. This scene popped into my mind because what this man did on the train achieved exactly the same effect. If there had been a substance in the air that would discolour because of tension, the air around him would surely have been turning dark blue very quickly, and everyone would have started to flee desperately. At that moment I realised that not only physical pollution exists when we flood our environment with garbage, but there is also psychological-spiritual pollution when the bad atmosphere we emit poisons the lives of others around us. In retrospect I am very grateful for boarding that train that day. It turned out to be a big lesson for me.

STORM-PROOF LOVE

Criteria for storm-proof communication

We will soon get back on that train; but, before that, let's look at the answers to the questions on the topic of communication given by the couples who are able to develop in the storm, as well as those who turn against each other in the storm and decline in their relationship:

Statement	Developing couples	Declining couples
I am very happy with the way we talk to each other.	79%	29%
My partner understands my feelings.	83%	36%
I can easily share my deeper feelings with my partner as well.	88%	47%
My partner is a very good listener.	80%	38%
My partner makes hurtful remarks about me.	6%	36%

As the table summarises well, the quality of our communication fundamentally determines the atmosphere of our relationship. If we feel that we are understood and we understand each other, then we develop a sense of belonging and comradeship. In this case, the difficulty will not turn us against each other, but vice versa; we will be the ones who become closer to each other against all the difficulties. This solidifies the 'us' feeling, which is manifested in trouble as 'the two of us, against the world'. And, if we can confirm this experience with our partner during a challenging time, it will be much easier for us to take on the next challenge, as we already have an empirical confirmation that our partner is on our side.

Communication and stress

The Swiss couple's therapist Guy Bodenmann has been researching the interactions between stress management and relationship communication for decades, and concluded that one of the biggest causes of relationship breakdown is the wrong response to stress. According to him, in such cases, the quality of communication deteriorates drastically, which weakens the couple's 'us' consciousness, which in turn implies that both partners begin to focus more on each other's disturbing traits. This will increase alienation and start the process of disaffection.[37] The formation and continued maintenance of the 'us' consciousness is critical. This causes us to define ourselves as a team in turbulent times. This enables us to treat challenges as something external, something that is outside of 'us', something that is our common enemy. If we lose this ability, challenges will easily become part of 'you', and from there it is only one step to saying: 'You are the problem!' Under the influence of Bodenmann's research, a study was conducted in which 41 couples were observed in a very stressful situation and analysed as to what personal pronouns they used in their conversations with each other, as well as whether the discussion was on a cognitive or an emotional level.[38] The study found that couples who use plurals ('we') instead of singular personal pronouns ('I' and 'you') have a much better chance of successfully dealing with stress, as well as those who engage not exclusively on an intellectual level, but also on an emotional level during the conversation.

> The formation and continued maintenance of the 'us' consciousness is critical. This causes us to define ourselves as a team in turbulent times.

Imagine that Maggie and Robby are arguing because Robby has misplaced the rubbish bin, and Maggie scratched the left front door of their car with the rubbish bin while parking. The conversation between the two of them goes as follows:

Robby: 'I can't believe you didn't see the rubbish bin sticking out and scratching the car. I think the repair will cost a fortune, but it could have been prevented if you had paid a little more attention.'

Maggie: 'You can't really think I did this on purpose to point out that you hadn't placed the bin properly into its place? Well, I cannot believe this! Really!'

Robby: 'OK, let's forget this issue! Anyway, the bottom line is that I always have to clean up your mess.'

But they could also discuss the problem this way:

Robby: 'I really feel sad that the side of our car is scratched so badly. It's annoying that a lot of our time will be consumed by the follow-up and all the waiting time until they're done painting. We really didn't need this now.'

Maggie: 'Oh, I must tell you, I feel terrible about it, too. I wish we had avoided this accident. Now we will pay an expensive fee, which will teach us to pay more attention and to be more careful about our belongings.'

Robby: 'Let's not allow this problem to overshadow our day. It's already happened: we can't change that. We will see a car repair shop next week, and we will see what can be done. Anyway, I wanted to show the chips on the bonnet to a painter as well, so we can have them fixed at the same time.'

Isn't it obvious how different the outcome of the second dialogue would be? (In the dialogues, some words are in the form of singular and plural addresses, and some involve intellectual and emotional approaches.) In the first, Robby and Maggie become opposing parties separated by the rubbish bin and the car. In the second example, however, the members of the couple are on the same side, facing the problem, the challenge. Here the car and the bin are not situated between them, but outside of their unit. For Robby, it's not Maggie who's the problem, but he and Maggie have a problem in common that they have to face together. And all this is done in a simple, easy-to-understand way with the means of human communication.

	Singular pronoun ('me', 'you')	Plural pronoun ('we')
Intellectual approach	Accusatory and defensive communication has no regard for emotions and can easily turn the parties against each other.	A logical and practical solution, together, without emotional involvement.
Emotional approach	Venting of negative emotions, deepening of grievances, escalation of conflict.	Preserving the community is more important than resolving the issue, strengthening the 'we' consciousness.

So, if you want to stay close to each other as a couple under stress, pay attention to two factors:

Good communication can do a lot to define the couple as a community, not as isolated, lonely individuals.

1. Use the personal pronoun 'we' instead of 'me' and 'you' (although it's still better to start the sentence with 'I' instead of getting carried away with 'you' messages);

2. Speak not only using your head (intellectual communication level) but also out of your heart (emotional communication level).

Of course, an intellectual approach can also have a positive effect if it helps the partner, for example, to get more information about the problem, directs attention to practical solutions, or provides usable advice. The emotional approach conveys empathy, solidarity, and understanding to the partner. It helps him to see what happened in a different light and has a calming effect on him, and is often accompanied by supportive physical gestures (for example, hugging or stroking).

Good communication can do a lot to define the couple as a community, not as isolated, lonely individuals; and when we are in a community, becoming 'us', our burdens are shared, and our resources are multiplied. Therefore, the systemic transactional model emphasises the interdependence and mutuality between partners,

The resources of one partner expand the resources of the other, creating new synergies. meaning that the stress of one partner always also affects the other one, but also that the resources of one partner expand the resources of the other, creating new synergies. This is true with regard to stress from daily hassles (for example, work stress) and more severe stressors (for example, dealing with a chronic illness).[39]

This process will then have beneficial effects on both the relationship and the individuals. Relationally, our 'we' consciousness is strengthened, and mutual trust, intimacy and reciprocity are strengthened; and, individually, our sense of mental and physical well-being, our relationship satisfaction, and our control of our lives also grows.[40]

The language of emotions

In the summary table, after the result for couples' overall satisfaction regarding their communication – 79% for developing couples, and 29% for declining couples, which is already a huge difference in itself – further important differences emerged in the expression and understanding of emotions as well. 'My partner understands my feelings' – 83% of developing couples agreed with the statement, but only 36% of declining couples felt the same. 'I can easily share my deeper feelings with my partner' – 88% of respondents in a developing relationship agreed with this statement, while only 47% of respondents in a declining relationship were able to say the same.

Andy was in deep trouble. He had made a few mistakes in his business, and he paid a desperate visit to his accountant to find out how to climb out of the pit. The waves crashed over his head: problems with the tax authorities, unpaid bills, and even his business partner demanding his money. He had gone through all of this, of course, without involving his wife in his decisions, radiating at home the image that everything was going well as usual. Zoe found out how much trouble was going on by accident, and at that moment she was sitting in front of me with Andy. The air was frosty around them, with Zoe reproachfully questioning her husband, who in turn gave answers that didn't move the matter towards a solution at all.

Zoe: 'You see, Gábor, the same thing is also going on at home. I ask something, and he just looks in front of himself or says a stupid thing that makes me explode.'

Andy: 'But what should I say? I've said a hundred times that I would do it differently now, but I don't know what to do. I will do my best to save the situation, but I cannot do more than that. It seemed like a great opportunity; I never imagined it was going to end up like this.'

Zoe: 'Gábor, reassure me that at least you understand what I'm talking about.'

Gábor: 'Andy, I think your wife doesn't like the fact that your answers come from the head, and not from your heart. She doesn't really need more information from you; she needs emotions. Because the information is very disturbing in this case, it forms a wedge between the two of you, but if you would share your feelings with your wife about the situation, it might draw you closer to each other. Would you try to tell her how you feel about all this?'

Andy: 'Well, I feel bad too; as you can imagine, it's not easy for me.'

Gábor: 'This is a good start; let your wife see into your heart a little deeper! Open your emotions to her. The trouble you're in is pretty big, but if your wife feels like you're not closing ranks with her in this trouble, but you exclude her from your emotions, it will only make the situation worse.'

Andy: 'But I never talk about my emotions – I'm not that type . . .'

I felt something needed to change. This man had no means of expressing his emotions. He never learnt how to connect with his own emotional world and how to make those emotions visible to the

> Zoe found out how much trouble was going on by accident, and at that moment she was sitting in front of me with Andy.

outside world. Sitting in front of me was a vibrant, influential, muscular man with dozens of people obeying his words, yet now he helplessly and powerlessly stared in front of himself because he didn't know what to do with this task. That's when I came up with an idea that might rescue him:

'Andy, do you feel like playing a game with me?'

Gábor: 'Andy, do you feel like playing a game with me? Imagine an emotional football game is going on inside your heart. Your wife and I don't see exactly what's going on in the match, but you are there in the commentary box and can see everything live. What if you were now our famous sport reporter, like Gábor Gundel Takács, a good sports reporter who has the special ability to make the match visible even on the radio for those who don't see it? Would you please cover the match for us in a live radio broadcast?'

Andy: 'Okay, we can try, but who are the players?'

Gábor: 'This is the best question you could ask. You see the players running on the field. Each player is an emotion. All you have to do is put the right names on the players' backs. Let's say instead of Ronaldo you call the player Frustration; instead of Messi it will be Fear; instead of Müller you call it Helplessness, and so on.'

Andy took the idea very well and produced an emotional opening that surprised his wife as well as me.

Andy: 'Well, let's see! A lot of players run back and forth on the field. One is Rage. I'm so angry at myself for getting into all this. I am angry with my business partner who dragged me into this and then turned against me. I also see another player, and it is Fear. I go to bed with a suffocating feeling in my throat every night because I'm scared. I'm afraid of punishment; I'm afraid of losing everything I've built up with so much hard work in previous years. I'm afraid of what people will think of me. And there's another player who is bigger than all the others on the football field. On the back of that, I would write Shame. He is two heads higher than all other players. [At this moment Andy buries his face in his hands and starts crying.] I am very ashamed of myself for putting you in a situation like this [he tells Zoe]. I wanted so badly to be a good husband to you, someone you can be proud of, someone you can look up to, in whose footsteps the kids want to follow. But now I feel like I've let down those I love the most and have no idea how to regain your trust. I am very ashamed of myself!'

My first shock was in seeing how Andy managed to open up his soul with the help of this simple analogy, and how he was able to connect with his innate emotional world. The second shock, however, was caused by Zoe's reaction. The woman who had looked at her husband with distant, hard eyes and spoken of him

As if sensing that the broken man now needed her strength, she hugged him, rested his head on her shoulders, and they sat together, crying together. It was a very moving scene!

in a critical, pungent style became emotional and hurried to the aid of her partner. As if sensing that the broken man now needed her strength, she hugged him, rested his head on her shoulders, and they sat together, crying together. It was a very moving scene! As Zoe pulled Andy's head over her shoulder, the man's face disappeared behind the woman, as if she were sending a message to him: 'You are safe here! I will save your face! Cry on my shoulder! We are one team.' Zoe's frustrated rage instantly turned into an understanding and protective love for her husband. And that was because her husband finally gave her (and me) a glimpse of his feelings. He finally spoke not from the head, but from the heart! As long as facts were debated, the accusing thoughts came, and the partners became defined as opposing parties. However, the emotions connected them. Andy's repetitive usage of the facts as excuses made Zoe more contemptuous and caused her to attack more viciously. However, an honest emotional opening-up activated compassion, co-operation, and protectiveness in her. She immediately got involved as a helper on her husband's side.

STORM-PROOF LOVE

Let me point out – partly in defence of men – that this road is terribly difficult for us as men. The longest journey in a man's life is when he walks from his head to his heart. A man's world is a ruthless place: a world in which weakness has no place, because if you look weak, you are pushed aside and might get humiliated or oppressed. And if we hear the message that expressing emotions is a weakness from an early age, then by our adulthood we will have absorbed it to such an extent that we will protect our emotions at all costs, and will pass this behaviour on to the next generation of men as a dreaded secret. This ensures that dysfunctional patterns are never lost, and therapists will always have work.

With this step, their relationship started to heal. As the saying goes, 'Revealing the feelings is the beginning of healing.'

I consider myself a great traveller. I have travelled to many distant parts of the world. I have travelled a long way – to Seattle, Cape Town, Beijing, Tokyo, and many other exciting places. But the longest journey, even for me, was from my head to my heart. I realised when I had to complete 150 hours of self-awareness to qualify as a family therapist: I am very happy to talk with anyone about their emotions in depth; however, my emotions are taboo. Today, I am very grateful that this has changed – and my wife and children are also happy about this.

Returning to Andy and Zoe, the sports reporter practice gave them a huge breakthrough, but then we took another bold step. The first step was that Andy – perhaps for the first time in his adult life at such depth – faced his emotions and learnt to express them. With this step, their relationship started to heal. As the saying goes, 'Revealing the feelings is the beginning of healing.' But then we took one more step towards emotional health. If you still remember to list the characteristics of an emotionally healthy person, then you know that it is not only about naming the emotions, but also about being able to control them. The case of Andy and Zoe became a real success story, because Andy learnt to master his emotions as well. To do this, we developed the football match analogy a little further and introduced a new element:

Gábor: 'Andy, that was amazing! You gave such an accurate broadcast of the match in your heart that I felt as if I were at the edge of the pitch and could see everything in front of me. Now I want you to get out of the commentary box and cross the edge of the field to the coach's stand. I ask that you not only tell me what you see on the field, but also take control and tell the players who shall do what on the field! Which player is most helpful at the moment, which one do you want to have a bigger role, and which one do you want to pull back onto the bench? Is there one player you would like to substitute with another?'

Andy: 'I like this! Shame is not a good advisor right now, because it paralyses me. I can't win a match if I don't dare to look into the eyes of others. What Zoe did to me fills me with hope, so

> 'I can't win a match if I don't dare to look into the eyes of others.'

now I bring Hope to the field! Now that I feel how much support Zoe gives, I have enough spiritual strength to face this whole thing. I believe I'm putting together a whole new team for myself: Hope, Determination, Gratitude. It's weird to say this, but at the moment I feel immeasurable gratitude. I can't tell you when I last felt so close to my wife. . . .'

I discovered this new technique completely by accident, but since then I have tried it with several pairs, and we have achieved similarly great results. A commentary box position helps men to connect with and name emotions, and a coaching position helps them to move forwards and regulate emotions. And all of this is reported on the spot for the partner, who becomes an even closer ally.

The art of listening

At the beginning of the chapter, the next item in the summary table was about listening: 'My partner is a very good listener.' Eighty percent of developing couples said yes to this sentence, compared to only 38% of declining couples agreeing with it. This fact confirms the old biblical wisdom: 'Everyone should be quick to listen, slow to speak and slow to become angry.'[41] I've covered a lot of techniques of listening in other volumes,[42] so I don't need to repeat them again, but I want to emphasise those that you absolutely need to keep your relationship on a growth trajectory in the storm, and also those which I haven't covered elsewhere yet. This is where everything I shared with you about

This fact confirms the old biblical wisdom: 'Everyone should be quick to listen, slow to speak and slow to become angry.'

mindfulness in the introductory chapter comes into play. Give your 100% attention! Stop the whole world and make your partner feel that all that matters is her or him: just as a secret agent registers every little detail, even if she doesn't see its full significance at the moment. Later, the image will come together, and the small details will find their

places, and our partner will feel that we have paid them special attention. At college, when I teach counselling, I usually tell my students that a good counsellor can be recognised by the ability to hear what the other party is just thinking about. Of course, this does not mean that in a good marriage we should start mind reading. I believe that the mere fact that a couple love each other doesn't mean they can figure out each other's thoughts. You don't even have to, either! But we may be able to give to our partner such attention that we can reach a depth of understanding that surprises them as well.

I met Dan Wile on an American study trip. (I just learnt while writing this book that he had died in March 2020. This made me really sad.) Dan had developed a brilliant couple's therapy technique that I am successfully applying myself. When I see that the partners don't understand each other, I sit next to them one by one and personify them. Somehow, I introduce the practice like this: 'Dear Joy, I am now sitting next to you for a while, and I'll try to articulate what I think your emotions say behind your words. In the meantime, I'll watch your reaction to see if I'm on the right track, but if you feel that I've missed your feelings, feel free to stop me and help out. Dear Steven, now your wife is speaking to you through my phone....' Then, based on the small pieces of information that Joy gave me in the form of words, gestures, sighs, and glances, I will tell him what I think is happening inside her. We experience magical moments when we hear our own feelings articulated by another person. This is a level of understanding we rarely receive in our lives. Just imagine how big an experience it would be for your partner if you gave her or him such an experience! Imagine how it would be if she felt that you paid attention to every little vibration, and you used every nerve you have to understand her. That's when miracles happen. I would like to draw your attention to one important thing! When you make an attempt to express what your partner might feel according to you, never do so in declarative mode, but always form it as a question! Instead of saying, 'I see you're very tense now, because one of the customers at the company made you upset again,' rather say, 'Do I see well, darling, that you are very tense now? Would you like to sit next to me and tell me what happened? Maybe someone at the company made you annoyed?' A statement is more like a judgement. You are like that, and

> We experience magical moments when we hear our own feelings articulated by another person. This is a level of understanding we rarely receive in our lives.

that's it! However, the question leaves several routes open. If we have managed to sense what is happening in our loved one, then our partner can confirm that we saw well, but if other feelings swirl in her, she has the opportunity to correct it without hurting the dignity of any of us.

The best to the most important!

At the end of this chapter about communication, let's get back to the train and the 'substance that turns the water blue' once again. In the research, only 6% of respondents in a growing relationship agreed with the statement, 'My partner makes hurtful remarks about me,' while 36% of those in a declining relationship agreed. Implicitly, since this is a negative sentence, the fewer the people who agree with it, the better. I would like to make a strong point here about the vocabulary couples use. I know very well that every language is extremely rich when it comes to swearing. I also know that our fathers and grandfathers and our mothers and grandmothers did the same. But, I beg you, why do we have to repeat something that didn't help them either? Did anything get better when they said something harsh? Did they get to love each other better because they told each other nasty words? I may be too conservative on this, but I am unwilling to get into the mainstream that exalts vulgarity. And it is terribly sad that different media (the most-read newspapers, movies, magazines, shows, and so on) that have a huge impact on people are uncritically accepted and give a platform to swearing in the public domain! No way! For my part, I resist this, and I represent this to the couples I work with . . . because it's not just a matter of taste. I am reminded of the case of Agnes and Peter. The couple said at our first meeting that they were very close to each other, the trust between the two of them was perfect, and they agreed at the beginning of their relationship that they would just get whatever was in their heart off their chest. And this would be voiced by constantly using ugly words about each other, words that eventually became uglier and uglier – all in the spirit of complete honesty, of course. Meanwhile, despite their 'perfect trust', their marriage was dying. You may wonder why? Of course, I cannot blame their condition solely on their style of conversation, but their hurtful words didn't go unnoticed. The rationale of their theory was that everyone sometimes thinks some ugly thoughts of each other in themselves anyway, so why not be honest enough to say them aloud? According to them, others lived on a lower degree of honesty because others didn't dare to say what they thought, because if they dared, they too would have talked ugly to each other. However, this theory is completely false. People in a good relationship don't even think about each other like this, and consequently don't even talk to each other using these words – so this kind of talk is not a manifestation of honesty, but of spiritual and

> I cannot blame their condition solely on their style of conversation, but their hurtful words didn't go unnoticed.

mental degradation. I can also explain this more scientifically. We construct our reality ourselves, and this construction takes place partly by our words. If we keep calling our partner stupid all the time, or naming him a pig, or naming her a cow and all sorts of other animals, we will sooner or later see the person as such – but it will also affect ourselves. The husband of a cow is an ox, not a wonderful, handsome, kind man. The wife of a pig is a sow, and not a beautiful, intelligent queen. So, as we talk about each other, it will result in seeing ourselves as such, and eventually it will define us. That's why we create worlds with our words and thoughts, and it matters immeasurably what we call into existence! So why not bring quality back into fashion in our oral communication?

> **People in a good relationship don't even think about each other like this, and consequently don't even talk to each other using these words.**

A lovely couple in their fifties sat in front of me. They had achieved everything in life that they ever wanted: a nice house, a pleasant holiday home, children who'd graduated from university, an expensive car, stylish clothes. . . . The husband loved to point out his accomplishments to me, as if he were just saying between the lines, 'Just because I'm sitting in couple's therapy for my wife's sake, don't think I'm any worse than you! I could control you; I eat people like you for breakfast. You had better look up to me and admire me, because I play in the top league, and you're only in the third division.' I felt the provocation in his words, and I felt like he wanted to drag me down to the level of his communication. He was annoyed that I didn't use any of the words he used – not even on his wife. To undo the tension that started to build up between us, I told him, 'Dear Robert! I have great respect for everything you have achieved. You could be a role model for many men in many ways. If I look at you, every detail is in its place; you belong in a league of your own. However, one thing seems to belie your situation. Everything represents a high quality in your life, except how you talk. It feels like a man wearing a Hugo Boss suit and a Calvin

STORM-PROOF LOVE

Klein shirt but having very cheap slippers on his feet. This doesn't seem to be your general standard!' The man fell silent and started to rethink his behaviour. His wife was very grateful afterwards that I had found a way to tell her husband something she had always wanted to tell him.

John Gottman is right: 'It means treating your spouse with the same respect you offer to company. If a guest leaves an umbrella, we say, "Here: you forgot your umbrella." We would never think of saying, "What's wrong with you? You are constantly forgetting things. Be a little more thoughtful, for God's sake! What am I, your slave to go picking up after you?" We are sensitive to the guest's feelings, even if things don't go so well. When a guest spills wine, we say, "No problem. Would you like another glass?" not, "You just ruined my best tablecloth. I can't depend on you to do anything right. I will never invite you to my home again." '[43]

> **We can sum up all this in a very simple way: we should use our most beautiful words and our kindest manners with those closest to us.**

We can sum all this up in a very simple way: we should use our most beautiful words and our kindest manners with those closest to us. If we can be kind to strangers even under pressure, let us give to our loved ones the best of us!

[37] Nina Heinrichs, Guy Bodenmann, Kurt Hahlweg, *Prävention bei Paaren und Familien* (Göttingen: Hogrefe, 2008), p. 32

[38] Kevin K. H. Lau, Ashley K. Randall, Nicholas D. Duran, Chun Tao, 'Examining the Effects of Couples' Real-time Stress and Coping Processes on Interaction Quality: Language Use as a Mediator', in: *Frontiers in Psychology*, 2019/9, pp. 31-44

[39] Guy Bodenmann, Ashley K. Randall, Mariana K. Falconier, 'Coping in Couples: The Systemic Transactional Model (STM)', in: M. K. Falconier, A. K. Randall, G. Bondenmann (ed.), *Couples Coping with Stress: A Cross-Cultural Perspective* (New York: Routledge, 2016), p. 8

[40] Ibid.

[41] James 1:19 (NIV)

[42] Compare: Gábor Mihalec, *Gyűrű-kúra: A sikeres házasság kézikönyve kezdőknek, házasoknak és újrakezdőknek* (Budapest: Harmat, 2019, third edition), pp. 69-90; also: Gábor Mihalec, *Ketten együtt magabiztosan: Párkapcsolat-építő kommunikáció* (Budapest: Kulcslyuk, 2013), pp. 42-52

[43] John M. Gottman, Nan Silver, *The Seven Principles of Making Marriage Work* (Random House, 2015), Kindle edition

Exercises

Pollutant emission test

On an imaginary scale, rate your partner along different aspects of mental environment protection. Put a mark on the scale where you currently see him, where 'zero emissions' means he doesn't harm the environment at all, and 'severely polluting' means he needs urgent change in that area! At the end, discuss how you classified each other.

←——————————————————————→
Zero emissions   **Kindness**   Severely polluting

←——————————————————————→
Zero emissions   **Attentivity**   Severely polluting

←——————————————————————→
Zero emissions   **Respect**   Severely polluting

←——————————————————————→
Zero emissions   **Courtesy**   Severely polluting

←——————————————————————→
Zero emissions   **Swearing**   Severely polluting

←——————————————————————→
Zero emissions   **Calmness**   Severely polluting

←——————————————————————→
Zero emissions   **Complaining**   Severely polluting

←——————————————————————→
Zero emissions   **Contentment**   Severely polluting

STORM-PROOF LOVE

Sports commentator exercise

Imagine that there is a football game going on in your emotional centre that your partner doesn't see, only you. Now give your partner live commentary of the match so he or she can 'see' the game based on what you say. The following questions will help you with this:

1. Who is on the field? Name the players, each player being an emotion.

2. Where did the players come from, and what are they doing?

3. In the current situation, how useful is what the players are doing on the field?

_____

_____

_____

_____

_____

_____

_____

4. Now change roles and act as a coach instead of a reporter. What kind of instruction do you give to the players to make the game useful for your relationship? Maybe you're taking someone off the pitch? Who are you sending on instead of that player?

_____

_____

_____

_____

_____

_____

_____

STORM-PROOF LOVE

Stress-reducing conversation[44]

Aim of the exercise: the couple learn to deal with an everyday source of stress outside their relationship (for example, the workplace).

Guideline: discuss a real-life stressful situation that is causing you tension (looming deadlines at work, a future event, and so on). The motto of the conversation is, 'Understanding comes first; advice comes last.' The main goal is for the listener to connect emotionally with the speaker and to understand him or her. You both need to try each role!

Speaker: talk about your stressful situation as deeply and in as much detail as you can.

Listener: provide support to your partner using the methods listed below. Avoid problem solving, and try your best to understand.

The support means that:
❋ You show real interest. Make eye contact. Ask questions.
❋ You are an ally of your partner. Show empathy.
❋ Communicate understanding: 'How tough!' 'Well, I'd also get upset by this, too.'
❋ 'It's us two against the whole world.' Don't take the side of the 'world'. Even if you agree with a third party, empathise with your partner's emotions. Focus on what your partner is feeling, not what he or she is doing.
❋ You show solidarity: 'This is our common problem, and we will face it together.'
❋ Provide tenderness and comfort: 'Come closer, and let me hug you. I'm completely on your side.'

Sharing emotions:

- Interest: 'Tell me more about this!' Ask questions.
- Excitement: 'Wow, that's tough stuff. Let's see!'
- Sadness: 'That is so sad.'
- Fear: 'Well, that would worry me too.'
- Anger and rage: 'Now I can see what upset you so much.'

Don'ts:

- Don't build a wall!
- Don't ignore your partner!
- Don't leave without reacting!
- Don't defend yourself!
- Don't criticise!

Questions you can ask:

First, ask, 'Do you feel understood?' If the answer is yes, you can ask if your partner wants to hear your advice or your opinion on the matter. If she or he says yes to that, tell him or her what you would do in this situation.

If the answer is no, continue with questions that will help you understand better:

- What hurts you the most in this situation?
- What bothers you most about this situation?
- What is the worst thing that could happen in this situation?
- How do you feel right now?
- Is there anything I could do to support you in this situation?
- What do you need?

Really strong couples have a twenty-minute stress-relieving conversation like this at the end of each day.

---

[44] John M. Gottman, Julie Gottman, *Treating Affairs and Trauma* (Seattle: The Gottman Institute, 2016), pp. 207, 208

STORM-PROOF LOVE

Conflicts – Keep Your Calm, Please!

During the lockdown, we went shopping every other week. There were masks on our noses, hand sanitisers in our pockets, and a disinfectant cloth in our bag to wipe the shopping cart we wanted to use. During one of our shopping trips, we listened to the radio in the car, and heard an interesting report featuring the leader of a helpline charity where abused women are supported. The lady stated that lately they had been facing double the usual number of calls, and I heard from her first the expression that the abusers had 'stepped up to a new level' during the lockdowns. This expression really stuck into my mind and made me take the topic of conflict management seriously. I had to examine it more closely.

The statements of the Couple's Check-up with the highest validity and reliability were used as the basis of our study here, as Professor Olson suggested at the time I wrote my doctoral research thesis:[45]

Statement	Developing couples	Declining couples
My partner is able to understand my opinions and ideas when we discuss problems.	78%	31%
Even during disagreements, I can share my feelings and ideas with my partner.	86%	45%
We are able to solve our disagreements.	89%	48%
We generally agree on ways to solve our disagreements.	68%	27%
My partner takes our disagreements seriously.	79%	44%
I remain calm even under emotional pressure.	46%	28%

The statements listed in the table ask about the broad spectrum of conflict management. They include thoughts and opinions (head), and also emotions (heart). They ask about the general culture of a couple's debate and how seriously the parties feel they are being taken during a disagreement. But what all this looks like in everyday practice – especially in a storm situation – I will explain in more detail soon.

Let's have a look at the bottom of the pot!

Ben and Agnes had already visited me twice. During these first two conversations they were very respectful and kind to each other, but I felt as if Agnes wasn't fully involved in the therapeutic work. Ben was much more motivated to change; he wanted to do something tangible to improve their marriage – but Agnes didn't seem to be fully involved in the process. However, I had a feeling that her passive attitude was not an indication of disinterest, but rather a defence. It felt as if she had already sustained some injuries and was now being very careful, letting herself get involved with cautious small steps into the process. Ben always gently let his wife go first at the door, acting like a real gentleman, but behind his kindness there was also some repressed temper. At the beginning of our third meeting, everything surfaced that Ben had tried to stifle before. He opened the door; burst into the room, visibly upset; sat down on the sofa without waiting for his wife; and began to say, 'Today will be our last meeting, and probably the last day of our marriage. I have had enough – no more! I put my heart and soul into this relationship for years, but I hardly got back anything in return. I don't think I'm such a bad partner that I should have to put up with this for even one more day. I'm angry at the way she treated me, and at myself for allowing it for this long. But I've learnt my lesson: no one will ever play with me again!'

> However, I had a feeling that her passive attitude was not an indication of disinterest, but rather a defence. It felt as if she had already sustained some injuries and was now being very careful.

STORM-PROOF LOVE

This performance was completely unexpected for me, since the man had always been very polite. However, Agnes was obviously not at all surprised. It felt as if she was all too familiar with it, as if she'd regularly been the target of similar outbursts at home . . . so I immediately understood what she was defending against with her seemingly passive, cautious attitude.

There were the three of us, sitting there, waiting for what would happen next. We didn't say a single word for a long time, but the gazes spoke more than a thousand words. Ben's eyes said, 'What do you say to that? I finally got it off my chest. I have spilled it out now.' And Agnes' gaze said something like, 'Here we are: now you see what I'm going through at home. So, should I be enthusiastic about how he plays the wounded heart here, while at home he keeps me in an emotional terror with his outbursts?'

> **We didn't say a single word for a long time, but the gazes spoke more than a thousand words.**

We sat in silence for a long time. After a while, holding the man's gaze, I asked, 'How do you feel, Ben? Has everything managed to come out?' The man, now somewhat reassured, said, 'Yes. Everything.' I wanted to lead him further in understanding what was just happening, so I said, 'I don't think everything came out. Actually, lots of things came out – just what matters was left inside. What I just saw here reminds me of the situation when someone is cooking soup and leaves the pot on the stove and the soup boils over. The hot liquid floods the stove, but that's not the essence of the soup. It's just the light, thin part from the top: but the real content, the hard stuff, stayed there at the bottom of the pot. What is left in you at the bottom of the pot? I have heard the accusations, but there must still be desires left at the bottom. Tell me and your wife your wishes too!'

The man was very surprised by this, and started thinking, then talking. 'I think what's still left inside me is my desire for recognition. I have been fighting so hard for this marriage. I have worked and continue to work so much for my family. It would be so good if Agnes could tell me that she saw, that she noticed how much I was doing for her; I'm so hungry for her to express her respect towards me. I would do anything for it!'

At that point, the atmosphere in the room changed completely. The former vibrating tension was replaced by a profound, inexplicable peace. Agnes switched from a defensive posture into an inquisitive, surprised, and sometimes supportive attitude. When I asked her how her husband's words affected her, to the shock of us all, she answered, 'I was just hoping, but I didn't know at all that he had this beneath the surface. This sounds quite different from when he is overboiling with anger. At those times, I would like to run far away from him. But now I would love to hug him and kiss him.' Hearing these words, Ben's eyes widened completely. He had just complained that his wife never wanted to hug him or kiss him, and now she said that's what she'd love to do most. I asked Agnes, 'What if you were to give in to this urge here and now, and really do what you wanted?' The result was a long hugging and kissing time there in my office, as if space and time around them had disappeared. It was just the two of them, and no one and nothing else. . . .

What just happened? We managed to bring to the surface what stays hidden in a lot of relationship fights. We see the surface – we hear loud and not so kind words, thoughts, opinions; sometimes we even hear a feeling or two ('I'm angry,' said Ben), but in the meantime the real motives and deepest needs, desires and fears remain hidden. The surface makes us turn against each other, but what happens at the deeper levels brings us closer together.

How do we know that a quarrel has deeper levels and isn't about what is stated? Morrie and Arleah Shechtman summarise the signs:[46]

- It feels like something is about to explode inside and wants to burst out. You feel like something bad is going to happen if you don't get it out of yourself.

- The intensity of the feeling is disproportionate to the circumstances. An outside observer would ask, 'What's the big deal about this; why should you get so angry?'
- The feeling resists interruption. Once the outburst has started, it seems unstoppable.
- You lose flexibility and openness. You can't even hear new approaches; you just repeat your own.
- You can recall similar emotional states from other relationships. Your frustration can spill over into general negative opinions about life, people, or the opposite sex.
- The intense emotional state prompts you to do things you later regret.

We see attacks, anger, and hurt, but it's really a coded language and hides a desperate struggle to restore the intimate connection.

When you experience these symptoms, start to suspect the problem. All that came out of you or your partner now was just the top layer of the soup, the thin and foamy liquid. But that's not the substance! What matters is down there at the bottom of the pot! Usually this is a deep desire to connect!

How strange, isn't it? We see attacks, anger, and hurt, but it's really a coded language and hides a desperate struggle to restore the intimate connection.

Sue Johnson really hits the nail on the head when she says, 'What couples and therapists too often do not see is that most fights are really protests over emotional disconnection. Underneath all the distress, partners are asking each other: "Can I count on you, depend on you? Are you there for me? Will you respond to me when I need, when I call? Do I matter to you? Am I valued and accepted by you? Do you need me, rely on me?" '[47]

I wish that everyone, when their partner stands in front of them angrily, with violent gestures, pushing their truth at high volume and endlessly listing their grievances, could see in front of their eyes in large, flashing letters, 'Your partner is desperately struggling to reconnect.' It was this realisation that turned Agnes back to Ben. This realisation broke Agnes' defensive retreat and prompted her to hug her husband and assure him in that embrace of her support, her availability, and the importance of their relationship. In recent years, I've walked the process with hundreds of pairs to get from the boiling foam of the soup to the real issues. In my book, *Marriage 2.0*, I likened this to the floors of a house that represent the process well (cellar = desires; garage = emotions; living room = behaviour). Since writing that book I have found that many couples can easily relate to the image of the pot and the boiling soup (thin, boiling liquid = accusations; the remaining stuff at the bottom of the pot = desires). The point is to look behind our partner's momentary behaviour and discover their deep-seated desires! Let's do the same for ourselves as well!

> **The point is to look behind our partner's momentary behaviour and discover their deep-seated desires! Let's do the same for ourselves as well!**

No matter how fierce and threatening the eruptions of one of the parties may seem, so far, without exception, it has been proved every time that there is, deep down, a desperate desire for reconnection. This desire has been articulated in many ways. Here are some examples of the most common desires:

- 'Do you love me, and can I trust that you won't withdraw your love from me even in difficult situations?'
- 'Can I trust you? Won't I be hurt if I open my heart completely to you?'
- 'Do you accept me and say yes to me the way I am?'
- 'Are you playing in my team? When the situation gets bad, will you close ranks with me, and not with someone else (for example, parent, child, brother, friend, lover, and so on)?'
- 'Are you my partner even when we see things differently?'
- 'Do you respect me and acknowledge and understand everything I do for you and for us?'

STORM-PROOF LOVE

My research made it unequivocally clear how important the ability to see deep beneath the surface is to ensure that couples do not turn against each other under pressure, but embrace each other to fight off the threat together. On the statement, 'When we argue, I feel that my partner understands my opinions and ideas,' 78% of respondents in a developing relationship said yes, but only 31% of those in a declining relationship said the same. This is a huge difference! The 'I can share my feelings and thoughts with my partner even when we don't agree' statement brings us even closer to the bottom of the pot. Here, the ratio between developing and declining pairs was 86% versus 45%! A lot is decided here! That makes the really big difference between the two directions!

How does this recognition turn into effective conflict management? By learning to relate to the content that lies at the bottom of our own pot, and to articulate it in a way that is understandable to our partner as well. In the meantime, we take great care that what we say is not offensive, insulting, or critical, as we do not want the other person to switch into offensive-defensive mode, but we want them to take a compassionate-cooperative stance towards us. And this can only be achieved by practising vulnerability instead of attacking. This is where the live coverage of the internal football game I wrote about in the previous chapter comes into play. Let's see how small things can cause big differences.

We want them to take a compassionate-cooperative stance towards us. And this can only be achieved by practising vulnerability instead of attacking.

'When you attack like this, I withdraw because I feel it makes no sense to argue with you. I want to talk to you in a calm atmosphere, but when you raise your voice, you hurt me, and I would rather lock myself in.' You might tell your partner this in a heated situation.

This wording is much better than Ben's outburst, as it contains several self-revealing expressions of emotions. However, if we take a closer look, we will understand why the recipient of this message will start a counterattack. The reaction is determined by the first several words: 'When you attack like this . . .' The wording will force the other party to defend or counterattack. How different would it sound if you said, 'When I feel attacked . . .'? With that, you've already taken the injury, and the other party will be able to continue to listen calmly without getting agitated. The phrase, 'When you raise your voice, you hurt me' once again pushes your partner into a corner. We managed to accuse each other of two things: screaming and insulting. This won't help the conversation either. We can articulate the phenomenon, but we need to try to keep the articulation of the emotional state in our own space instead of blaming each other. For example, 'When you raise your voice, I feel deep pain and close up.' While the first wording pressed the attack-defence button in your partner's head, even if it expressed emotions, this version is sure to appeal for cooperation:

> **We managed to accuse each other of two things: screaming and insulting.**

'When I feel attacked, it makes me retreat because I start to struggle to see if it all makes sense. I want to be able to talk about everything in a relaxed atmosphere, but when you raise your voice, I feel deep pain and close up.'[48]

The difference looks very tiny, but the effect will be hugely different compared to the previous wording. This principle is so universal that the wording of our attempt to resolve the dispute makes the result predictable. According to John Gottman's statistical analysis, the outcome of a 15-minute debate can be predicted with 96% accuracy based on the first three minutes.

'But we haven't done this before!' 'But it's so artificial and strange.' 'We already have a well-established method that we can't just simply overwrite.' 'I'm the type who . . .'

Don't even try, as I've heard so many excuses that I could recount the full list even in my dreams. Please don't take as disrespectful what I'm just about to write. These excuses are just nonsense! If something can be done better, then let's do it better! I understand that change requires difficult and conscious choices, but I can't accept doing something in a given (bad) way for the rest of our lives just because we're used to it. It is true that this might be a different language than

These excuses are just nonsense! If something can be done better, then let's do it better!

what you may have spoken so far – but you can learn it! It's like buying your first automatic car after many years of driving with manual transmission. In the first few weeks, you will have to constantly remind yourself not to use your left foot and not to feel for the clutch, and not to try to keep your hand on the gearstick.

The same will also happen with your new conflict-management style. At first you need to constantly remind yourself not to attack, but to express feelings and desires, and not to give in to the old routine; and, in the meantime, you will make mistakes! When I switched to an automatic car, I stepped on the brake a few times with my left foot, thinking I was pushing the clutch, and I was almost bumped from behind – there was some swearing and a fist shaking from behind. But, after a while, you don't have to remind yourself any more. The new method will take hold and will become the new norm! You have to wait for this point, and you will have to have a greater need for self-discipline only until then.

Violence is not the solution – NEVER!!!

Let's go back a bit to the topic I started this chapter with. While authorities in ninety countries around the world have ordered partial or full lockdowns to keep the population safe, for many families, the same thing that should have provided protection became the greatest danger. Countless women and children (and some men) got trapped in the same space as their abuser. The phenomenon grew so big that the UN called the wave of violence in homes a shadow epidemic alongside the coronavirus pandemic.[49]

Unfortunately, the story of John and Susie is typical of several families during this period. The couple with two children in their early thirties were suddenly overwhelmed by the tide of changes. One week they were still living their normal lives; the next week the little schoolboy and the kindergarten-age child had to stay at home, John was working from home, and Susie's job became completely precarious, so she was sent home on unpaid leave. Any one of these changes is enough to stall the functioning of an average family and necessitate a complete replanning – but all these changes in one package were too much for them. Susie's self-esteem was affected by not earning any money, and home-schooling with their older son overworked her nervous system. Of course, the little one also hung around her all day, and John – rightfully so, according to him – withdrew from the front line of family life, because, as he often said during this period: 'Someone has to make money.' The atmosphere in the home became more and more tense; they talked to each other more and more harshly, with more and more insensitivity; and they needed more and more drinks in the evenings to be able to fall asleep. The number of gentle touches decreased, and the word 'sex' was removed from everyday use. Then it happened one Thursday night. The quarrel that had started out of a frosty mood escalated and became very intense, and then crossed a point they had never dared to cross before. They had always stopped in their previous fights, because they didn't want to hurt each other. Now, however, they crossed this point. The dignity of the other no longer mattered: it didn't matter if the kids woke up or the

> In the heat of anger, Susie felt that all her arguments had run out, and she could no longer pull anything out of her imaginary trick box, and in the heat of the moment she hit John.

neighbours would hear it. One thing mattered: getting rid of the tensions and winning the battle. And it happened. In the heat of anger, Susie felt that all her arguments had run out, and she could no longer pull anything out of her imaginary trick box, and in the heat of the moment she hit John. John was visibly shocked. This had never happened before in their relationship. They both felt that they had crossed a line, but John would have felt weak and cowardly if he had not responded to this rough strike, so he pressed Susie against the wall and yelled into her face at full volume.... The next day they called me to help them clean up the mess so they could find each other again, because, 'Even though we crossed a border, we are not beasts. At the end, we love each other.'

The situation was quite different with Levi and Mary. Unfortunately, violence was not unknown to the couple with three children of similar age as the previous family. Levi is a very nice, good-looking, intelligent man, but his wife said he used to become unpredictable every other month. At such times, **no matter what was happening at home, or how intimate they were,** he provoked his family until he found someone to pour his anger on. Many times, this someone was Mary; sometimes it was a child; and it also happened that several family members became targets at the same time. Most of the time this happened at home late at night, so Mary heroically sacrificed herself to protect the children, but after that she had to hide the bruises on her arms or face for days, lying to the neighbours about what the loud noise was the night before. But it had happened in the shopping centre, and once even in the car park of a petrol station. On the most recent occasion, Levi wasn't bothered by the fact that the ugly incident was witnessed by others. At this point Mary had had enough. Gathering her last drops of courage, she announced that she was unwilling to live like this any more, and decided that she needed to protect herself and her children from her husband's unpredictable outbursts of anger. After the fights, Levi was always remarkably kind, brought flowers to Mary, and took the children to the playground, obviously trying to compensate – but he never apologised. When abuse was discussed in a sober, emotional state, he always made others responsible. 'If the naughty kid had gone to brush his teeth in time when I told him to, I wouldn't have punished him.' 'If dinner had been ready in time, I wouldn't have had to discipline you.' By the time of the last occasion, however, Mary had lost her confidence and was constantly afraid in his presence.

I guess, even for those who are not professionals, it's easy to recognise that the two types of abuse are completely different. The literature calls one type (John and Susie's case) situational abuse, and the other (Levi and Mary's) characterological abuse.[50]

In the case of characterological abuse, the roles are strictly defined: there is the perpetrator, and there is a victim (or several victims). The perpetrator is always the same person (in heterosexual relationships it is generally but not exclusively the man). The characterological abuser uses his muscle strength, his physical superiority, to control the family. He does not take responsibility for the abuse, but rather blames others. The victim, on the other hand, typically has no influence on the abuser's behaviour. Whatever the victim does, the abuser will always find a reason to exert abusive behaviour. Abusive behaviour can have serious consequences, resulting in serious injury or even in death. In most cases, the perpetrator does not show regret and doesn't apologise for what he did.

> He does not take responsibility for the abuse, but rather blames others. The victim, on the other hand, typically has no influence on the abuser's behaviour.

The story is different in the case of situational abuse. Such abusive behaviour is a consequence of emotional and physiological flooding (I will explain this term in more detail later). In this case, both parties resort to violence; however, in most cases it does not cause serious injury. While characterological abuse is more common among men, in 71% of cases of situational abuse, women take the first step and men reply in kind.[51] Situational abusers take full responsibility for their actions and feel deep regret for them. They work together to find a solution and do everything they can to change the situation.

Now that you can clearly distinguish between these two types of abuse, the following question may come up: 'What can be done?'

STORM-PROOF LOVE

The answer varies from country to country, depending on what the law says. In the US, for example, in 31 of the 50 states, any couple's therapy intervention is legally prohibited if abuse is present in the relationship. In other countries there is no such legal prohibition, but it is emphasised in therapists' training: if there is abuse, there is no therapy. However, John Gottman believes this picture should be further nuanced. In the case of situational abuse, abuse is not the main problem, but rather 'only' a symptom of a deeper personal or relationship problem. And if the cause is treated, the symptom will also disappear. However, caution is fully justified in the case of characterological abuse. It can happen that the victim's request for help and attempt to get therapeutic help will make the abuser more violent, starting a worse cycle of violence than the previous ones: and, obviously, no therapist wants to risk that. In such a case, the aim must be to keep the victim safe so that the abuser cannot continue to terrorise them; and the abuser must participate voluntarily in therapy in order to process whatever needs to be addressed. During therapy, it often turns out that the abuser is a victim himself: for example, he is the victim of his parents' violence and carries on deeply internalised patterns that he has learnt from them. However, dealing with this is the individual's responsibility and cannot be passed on to the spouse or children.

> **Caution is fully justified in the case of characterological abuse. It can happen that the victim's request for help and attempt to get therapeutic help will make the abuser more violent.**

In our research, a clear difference emerged concerning abusive behaviour between developing and declining couples. Moreover, even slight differences between the sexes can be found. To the statement, 'The confinement made me verbally or physically rude to my partner,' 7% of developing couples said yes (and, among those, 6% of women said yes, and 11% of men), but 32% of declining couples said yes (and, among those, 22% of women said yes, and 21% of men). The inverted statement of the same subject yielded an interesting result: only 3%

of respondents in a developing relationship said yes to: 'During the pandemic, my partner was verbally or physically rude to me' (as if they were more critical of themselves than their counterparts), compared with 25% of those in a declining relationship. It's interesting to look at the sex ratios again. Among those in a declining relationship, 25% of women agreed, compared to 32% of men. Although we do not have specific information on the exact nature of the abusive behaviour, it is suspected that this figure confirms the hypothesis that in situational abuse mostly women make the first move, which is then reciprocated by men.

Abuse is a completely zero-tolerance issue!

Abuse is a completely zero-tolerance issue! For people who are not committed to each other, even at the faintest sign of abuse, I advise, 'Break up and leave now!' This is not to say that abuse should be tolerated in the slightest in marriage. However, it is true that in a marriage the parties go further for each other, and they usually do not terminate the relationship immediately, but tend to search and develop a solution with more commitment.

Maintaining calm even when the waves crash overhead

Anyone who knows us more personally knows that we are big pet lovers. We love animals, and we have kept and keep many kinds of pets, but for us it is also equally important that we care for all animals with competence and responsibility. I'm usually the one in our family who reads everything about the species before we enrich our zoo with a new animal.

That's how it happened when my son came up with the idea that he wanted a dog: namely, a pug. I bought the book of a famous dog expert and started reading. I was shocked by Cesar Millan's description of why some dogs will go totally nuts next to their owners. Success lies in the behaviour – or perhaps, rather, in the attitude – that Millan calls 'calm and assertive'. 'One dog can assert dominance over another by simply moving in with calm, assertive energy and claiming the space. . . .' Humans do have words, though, and we rely on them, whether we are communicating in conversation or in writing. Because of our intellectual capacity for speech, it is very easy for us to lose touch with our own energy, and to have no idea what we are projecting to the world. . . . 'To be successful as the pack leader – and as a person in general – you need to be mindful of your energy and learn to adjust it when you are not in a calm, assertive mode.'[52] These few sentences answered the question of why we meet so many misbehaving dogs on the streets and in the parks. Well, it's because the owner is also misbehaving. The dog takes on the 'energy' (in human language: the emotional radiation) of the pack leader. So, if I want Roxi to be calm, I have to stay calm too. The dog is a great mirror for the emotional radiation of its owner.

Then came our horses. First came Mimóza, then Royal. Once again, I followed my trusted method. I looked for literature from the most renowned individuals in this field. That's how I came across Monty Roberts, the horse whisperer. I started reading his book, and it felt like he must have talked to Cezar Millan.[53] He, too, kept stressing calmness. 'Stay calm!' repeated the book over and over again. Why? Because the horse also reflects the emotional radiation of its rider. If the rider is nuts, then the horse will also be nuts. Only, a horse going nuts will have a much higher consequence than our little pug Roxi's misbehaviour. Roxi can't do much harm to us with her 9 pounds and tiny teeth. However, a 1,100-pound horse can kill a human, even if she doesn't intend it at all – so we had to learn to calm down before we got close to the animal. Project calm emotional radiation in all circumstances.

Why? Because the horse also reflects the emotional radiation of its rider. If the rider is nuts, then the horse will also be nuts.

According to my research, this is the hardest. Even among developing couples, only 46% agreed to the sentence, 'I am able to keep my calmness even in an emotionally stressful situation.' For declining couples, the rate was only 28%. We learn more about this phenomenon by looking at the gender ratios of respondents in the developing relationship: of those, 45% of women and 53% of men answered yes. Among couples with declining relationships, however, an even greater difference emerged. Only 25% of women and 45% of men in this group answered yes to the above statement. Even if both sexes have something to learn in this area, it seems that men have a better ability to remain calm even in an emotionally heated situation.

Why is this so important? What happens to us when we get tense? Emotional flooding (scientifically: diffuse physiological arousal, or DPA) experienced during relationship quarrels was described by John Gottman and his colleague, Robert Levenson. They discovered DPA in their research 'when they measured what was happening to some couples as they escalated during quarrels. In the middle of conflict-related discussions, partners who flooded might look slumped, passive, and quiet, but internally their hearts were racing at over 100 beats per minute. Their blood pressure was skyrocketing; their respiration, shallow and quickening; and their skin, perspiring. In short, they were being hijacked by cortisol and the adrenaline-fuelled fight-or-flight response, an appropriate reaction to being attacked. Flooding was blocking them from thinking clearly, addressing problems creatively, accessing their empathy and humour, and hearing their partner's words accurately. Flooding was also producing tunnel vision and hearing that mistranslated any messages they perceived into signals of attack.'[54] Maintaining calm is therefore critical when pursuing conflict management with a positive outcome. The long-voiced principle of the 'need to vent the anger' would not only be unhelpful in reducing the tension, but would be explicitly harmful! This is because the emotionally overwhelmed parties begin to think very negatively about each other, which is expressed in their destructive verbal attitude, which in turn puts an immeasurable strain

> **It seems that men have a better ability to remain calm even in an emotionally heated situation.**

on their relationship.[55] So how can we be of help, then? By venting out the tension, or by suppressing it and hiding it inside of ourselves?

I remember studying psychology at a university in Germany, and one of my teachers once invited me to his private practice to see what his office looks like. Dóri and I visited a state-of-the-art psychological practice in Hanover. I was impressed that every kind of therapeutic procedure had its own room. He had a separate room for individual adult therapy (consolidated, with serious furnishings), another room where he worked with children (coloured walls, with children's furniture and soft toys), and there was also an interesting room whose function I couldn't discern at first. When I entered, my feet sank into a very soft floor. When I leaned against the wall, I felt my hand sink into the sponge-like wall. The furnishing was very simple: some boxing gloves, foam bars and headgear. Answering my puzzled expression, my teacher said that this was the rage room, where couples could take their anger out on each other and could even hit each other safely. Today we already know that this is harmful! Fuming is not good for a relationship. It floods, leading to more grievances that need to be addressed in newer fights. This is not to say that suppression would be better. Not at all! Instead of suppression and venting, we need to learn to channel and transform our anger. At this point, all that I explained about resilience, mindfulness, and emotional health will be beneficial.

Fuming is not good for a relationship. It floods, leading to more grievances that need to be addressed in newer fights.

It helps a lot if – despite the tension – we consciously pay attention to our breathing and we breathe slowly and deeply into our abdomen, not into our chest. Also pay attention to your voice, as we instinctively switch to a higher volume, a higher tone, and a faster speech tempo when we are nervous – but you can consciously prevent all of this by speaking more quietly, deeply, and slowly, even in a tense situation. Also, remember to use the word 'we' many times, emphasise your emotions, and avoid any offensive gestures.[56]

Conflicts – Keep Your Calm, Please!

Remember, the debate is never won by the one who is more angry, who shouts more loudly, or who hits more forcefully. The debate is won by those who can remain calm even in the storm, and who can also help their partner to calm down. This is what Jesus also teaches in the Sermon on the Mount: 'Blessed are the peacemakers, for they will be called the children of God.'[57]

---

[45] The statement 'I remain calm even under emotional pressure' is not part of David Olson's questionnaire; it is my addition.

[46] Morrie and Arleah Shechtman, *Love in the Present Tense: How to Have a High Intimacy, Low Maintenance Marriage* (Boulder: Bull, 2004), pp. 124-125

[47] Sue Johnson, *Hold Me Tight! Seven Conversations for a Lifetime of Love*, Kindle edition

[48] John M. Gottman, Nan Silver, *The Seven Principles of Making Marriage Work*, Kindle edition

[49] Shadow pandemic – see: Phumzile Mlambo-Ngcuka, 'Violence against women and girls: the shadow pandemic', source: *https://www.unwomen.org/en/news/stories/2020/4/statement-ed-phumzile-violence-against-women-during-pandemic* (accessed: 31/8/2020)

[50] Julie Schwartz Gottman, John M. Gottman, *10 Principles for Doing Effective Couples Therapy* (New York: W. W. Norton, 2015), pp. 52-57

[51] Ibid.

[52] Cezar Millan, 'Short Guide to a Happy Dog' (*National Geographic*, 2013), pp. 58, 59

[53] Monty Roberts, *The Man who Listens to Horses* (Random House, 1997), Kindle edition

[54] Julie Schwartz Gottman and John M. Gottman, *10 Principles for Doing Effective Couples Therapy*, pp. 86, 87

[55] Clifford Notarius, Howard Markman, *We Can Work It Out: How to Solve Conflicts, Save Your Marriage, and Strengthen Your Love for Each Other* (New York: Perigee, 1994), pp. 172-173

[56] In my book *Marriage 2.0* I share more methods. See: Mihalec Gábor, *Házasság 2.0 – a kapcsolatot cseréld, ne a társad!* (Budapest: Harmat, 2018), pp. 88-91

[57] Matthew 5:9, NET

STORM-PROOF LOVE

Exercises

What's at the bottom of the pot?

Think of a recent conflict situation between you and your partner that went badly (you can even do the exercise together). As in the pot example above, think about what you said that made the conversation go in the wrong direction (the overboiling liquid of the soup). Think also of what was left at the bottom that didn't boil out, especially if it was good and helpful for your partner to know and hear, but you couldn't find the way to express it.

Now rewrite your part of the dialogue in a way that will help both of you in the ensuing conversation. Focus on communicating your desires and emotions, and erase anything that could be depicted as an accusation, reproach, or criticism by your partner. Write your new dialogue here:

_____

_____

_____

_____

_____

_____

Not with me!

The following questions may evoke painful memories for you. Do this exercise only if you are in a calm, predictable and safe environment. The purpose of the exercise is to make you aware of whether abuse is present in your relationship, and, if so, to find help to process it.

Below are some questions to help you better articulate what is going on between you. Please think about them and contact a professional for help if necessary. If abuse is not present in your relationship (I sincerely hope it isn't), simply skip this and move on to the next exercise.[58]

❀ Has there ever been any unwanted, unpleasant, or frightening physical contact between you and your partner?

❀ If so, what exactly happened? What did that trigger in you?

❀ How often does this happen? What triggers the process? When was the last time it happened?

❀ Have you ever suffered an injury during an event like this? Have you ever needed medical care after such an event?

❀ Are you afraid of your partner?

❀ Have you ever talked to your partner about this? If so, how did he or she react? Did your partner take responsibility for his/her behaviour, or did he/she blame you for it?

❀ Have you ever considered leaving in order to protect your own and your children's physical safety?

❀ Has your partner ever forced you to have sex?

You can find more help here:
www.womensaid.org.uk
www.mankind.org.uk

You can also call your local emergency number – in the UK, it's 999.

---

[58] Source of the questions: Julie Schwartz Gottman, John M. Gottman, *10 Principles for Doing Effective Couples Therapy*, pp. 55, 56

STORM-PROOF LOVE

Calm down, and keep calm

This exercise will help you keep your heart rate below 100 and not fall victim to the 'fight or flight' response (DPA). Do it in a calm, peaceful environment, in a calm and sober state!

1. What has been the roughest, scariest, or most stressful relationship situation for you in the past year?

_____

_____

_____

_____

_____

2. What reactions did this situation provoke in you?

Physical reactions: _____

_____

_____

_____

_____

Feelings: _____

_____

_____

_____

_____

Thoughts:_____

_____

_____

_____

_____

Deeds:_____

_____

_____

_____

_____

3. List at least five alternatives to keep yourself calm in the next similar situation.

_____

_____

_____

_____

_____

4. Keep this list within reach, and if another stressful situation develops, go through these alternative solutions!

STORM-PROOF LOVE

'To Reproduce In Captivity'
– Sex and Tenderness Under Pressure

The lockdown brought very strange things out of us. It brought to the surface traits of our personality that we hadn't known or had imagined differently. Lockdown provided quite a few surprises in the area of sexuality as well.

Isabelle said that, before the coronavirus hit, she had a completely normal, healthy sex life with her husband, Adam. They were together 2-3 times a week and really enjoyed their intimacy. They both felt a need for it, and they both considered gentle co-existence as their common resource. However, something changed during the pandemic. The constant stress, the lifestyle changes due to the restrictions, and the anxiety about their elderly parents affected Isabelle's libido. Adam still had his sexual needs, but Isabelle felt no sexual desire any more, and even reacted in a hostile manner to her husband's advances. After another failed attempt, she jokingly said to Adam, 'You need to understand, I am a species that does not reproduce in captivity!'

For Emma, completely the opposite happened. Before the crisis, she rated her own sexual appetite as average, but during lockdown her sexual drive accelerated – she was constantly craving sex. She wanted to make love with her partner 4-5 times a week, instead of the previous once-a-week frequency. Thomas was very impressed at first, but after a while he started to run out of energy. During one of our conversations, he noted, 'As a result of the pandemic, I revised my previous decision and decided to marry Emma.'

During lockdown her sexual drive accelerated – she was constantly craving sex.

His statement sounded very solemn and serious, so I asked with interest what had made him change his mind. He replied, with a cheeky smile, 'All my friends have reported a drastic reduction in sex after they married. I can't keep up the pace any more with her, so let marriage come!'

I hope these two humorous but very real-life experiences have prepared you to deal with another sensitive topic. Sexual intimacy is the next important pillar of storm-proof love. The research revealed that there is a significant difference between developing and declining couples in this area as well.

Statement	Developing couples	Declining couples
I am completely satisfied with the amount of affection my partner has shown.	78%	32%
Our sexual relationship is satisfying and fulfilling.	78%	35%
My partner blackmails or punishes me with sex.	1%	9%
My partner shows sexual interest in me.	89%	57%
I have full trust in my partner's sexual fidelity.	95%	80%

The biggest difference exists at the question of quantity. The statement 'I am completely satisfied with the amount of affection my partner has shown' was answered positively by 78% of developing couples, but only by 32% of declining couples. This is in itself a compelling difference, but, when combined with the statements 'My partner shows sexual interest in me' and 'My partner blackmails or punishes me with sex' questions, we get an even more detailed picture. Couples in a storm-proof relationship are content with the amount of expression of physical tenderness, do not use sex manipulatively to influence each other in the relationship, and regularly show interest in each other. The gender ratios of responses seem to support the stereotype that men are more willing to have sex and feel less sexually accepted in their relationship than women. The statement 'I am completely satisfied with the amount of tenderness my partner has shown' does not show a significant difference between women's and men's responses, but the other two do. While 18% of men in a declining relationship felt that their partner was blackmailing or punishing them with sex, only 8% of female respondents felt the same way. The difference is even greater at the third question. Even among women in a declining relationship, 60% felt that their partner was interested in them sexually. In contrast, only 34% of men in a declining relationship felt that their partner was sexually interested in them. This question produced a difference among respondents living in a developing relationship, even if it wasn't as big as among those in a declining relationship. Here, 91% of women and 75% of men answered yes. In other words: 25% of men in a developing relationship and 66% of men in a declining relationship felt that their partner was not showing sexual interest in them. This is a significant number. Many of them could identify with Robert, whose painful voice still rings in my ear: 'Gábor, can you imagine what it is like to live constantly in a state of sexual starvation for years? Well, that's what I live in!' I remember just as sharply the struggle of Matthew, who put it this way: 'Sex is not important for my wife. She could live smoothly without it. But it feels like living hell for me after two weeks of deprivation. I can't sleep, I feel anxiety in my stomach, I can't pay attention to my work – and, besides, I could work around the problem, and I could get sex elsewhere. I could spend a lot of money without my wife ever noticing. But I love her!' Of course, I could also tell you about Petra, Anita, and the many other women who have already been driven to the brink of despair by their husbands' sexual apathy, but, statistically, this problem seems to affect men more than women. Let's add one more aspect to the subject. Just as the most important need for women in

> **Just as the most important need for women in a relationship is emotional security, so men's greatest desire can be summed up in two simple items: less quarrelling, and more sex.**

a relationship is emotional security, so men's greatest desire can be summed up in two simple items: less quarrelling, and more sex.[59] On either side, one of the most painful experiences of our lives is to lie in the closest physical proximity to your spouse while struggling with the feeling that the person doesn't desire you, doesn't want you, doesn't want to be close to you. More couples need to work on this than you would imagine.

Sex, stress, and porn

We have known since ancient times that sex has a stress-reducing effect; and, vice versa, stress also affects our sexual desires. Some people experience increased sexual drive under stress, and others experience a decrease. We need to be sensitive and attentive to this difference if we want a storm-proof marriage. Both reactions are considered normal – there is nothing pathological

> We have known since ancient times that sex has a stress-reducing effect; and, vice versa, stress also affects our sexual desires.

or abnormal about it. The phenomenon occurs in both sexes; although, statistically, women appear to be more likely to move towards a decrease in desire,[60] while men tend to move towards an increase. Naturally, it is easier for the couple if their desire changes in the same direction, but often partners start to change in opposite directions. This, in turn, can generate further conflict, uncertainty, and emotional distancing.

Sex, when it happens, has several beneficial biochemical effects on stress. It increases endorphin production, which fills us with a sense of happiness, and this in turn stimulates the increase of dopamine, a very potent neurotransmitter that triggers physical and mental well-being. At the same time, stress hormone (cortisol) levels decrease. Further beneficial effects are that, during orgasm, our brain releases hormones (oxytocin in women, vasopressin in men) that strengthen the bond to our partner, and it increasingly forges the couple into an 'us' from two individuals.

A number of health-protecting and stimulating effects are also attributed to sex. A study by the Wilkes University of Pennsylvania found that people who had sex 1-2 times a week had 30% higher levels of immunoglobin A (IgA) than those who had intimacy less or more frequently – it seems that too much sex is not useful either.[61] Immunoglobin A is an antibody that plays a significant role in fighting disease. A regular and satisfying sex life has a protective effect against cardiovascular problems appearing in older age.[62]

A regular and satisfying sex life has a protective effect against cardiovascular problems appearing in older age.

During the lockdown, several couples approached me with the question of how to survive the weeks when they must be physically separated from each other. There were some whose partner worked abroad and got stranded there, and there were others who, because of their studies, were in separate cities and could not enjoy each other's physical touch. Many have turned towards porn in this situation. During the pandemic, the traffic of porn sites increased by 11.6% worldwide, prompting some paid sites to make their content free during lockdown, leading to an explosive increase in porn consumption (57% in Italy, 38% in France and 61% in Spain).[63] However, this opportunity should be treated with extreme caution, as oxytocin and vasopressin produced during orgasm not only strengthen our attachment to our partner, but can also increase our attachment to the screen, masturbation, or even various objects (fetishes), and what was previously a positive attachment towards our partner can become a negative attachment called addiction. Gottman notes that, while the simultaneous use of porn by a couple (for stimulation purposes) carries less of a risk of addiction, it still has a detrimental effect by instilling false ideas in the couple's thoughts about sex, compared to which their own intimate lives would appear always under-stimulated, boring, and inferior; and, in relationships where one partner has a porn addiction, one party will completely lose interest in shared sexual experiences in 70% of couples.[64]

Rejection can also be an intimate experience

No, this subtitle is not a call to masochism! I have observed during many therapeutic conversations that sex has become such a taboo that the mere utterance of the word causes the couple to get tense. I found a way to unravel this paralysing condition, which often torments couples for years, by helping them to articulate what sex really means to them. That is, what do they really need when they say they need sex? As Peter Rutter puts it in his classic book, 'Sexual intercourse is the ultimate symbol of intimate human relationship. The act of intercourse can allow us to experience in the most intense way possible our deepest biological, emotional, and spiritual strivings, and at the same time allow us to share these feelings with another person. . . . Sex can be an act, but it can also be a highly meaningful metaphor.'[65] Sex is a metaphor or symbol of some deeper need, but many times it remains hidden from the individual what that deeper need is. If a person learns what sex means, first for themselves and then for their partner, in the deepest sense, then they will be able to reject sexual advances when they don't feel like having sex in such a way that rejection itself becomes an intimate experience. This way both sides will benefit. The partner who does not want sex at a given moment does not have to go along with it against their desires, and the partner who wants sex will receive the affirmation that sex itself would have given. Let me use some examples to illustrate what I mean.

> **Sex is a metaphor or symbol of some deeper need, but many times it remains hidden from the individual what that deeper need is.**

- Anna is really hurt when Gabriel refuses to have sex with her. She feels at those moments that her femininity got wounded. He feels humiliated and pushed aside. Digging deeper into her childhood stories, we learn that his father never knew what to do with her. He was expecting a boy, but got 'only' a girl instead. As a little girl, she did everything she could to get her father's attention, yet she can't recall a case when her father said that he loved her, or stroked her hair, or took her in his lap. As an adult woman, every time she tried to draw Gabriel's attention to herself with a sexual overture, she really wanted to receive confirmation that her husband loves and values her and considers her a woman. For her, sex is a metaphor for accepting and confirming her femininity. When Gabriel is tired and doesn't want to have sex, he calls into question Anna's femininity. The couple were relieved when they learnt how to separate the two issues. From that moment on, Gabriel hasn't simply been declining sex, but has been saying: 'Honey, I am the luckiest guy on this planet to have such a wonderful woman as my wife. You are the most beautiful to me, and I am very proud to have a wife that others can only dream of. I'm very tired to have sex at the moment, but I'd love to fall asleep as we cuddle and feel the warmth of your body.' After hearing this, Anna's desire for confirmation is fulfilled, and Gabriel doesn't have to say yes to sex at all costs, even though he has no wish to have sex at that moment. Of course, he cannot abuse this by refusing every initiative from now on with his newly learnt technique.

After hearing this, Anna's desire for confirmation is fulfilled.

- The situation is similar for Ben, whose family was left by his mother for another man when he was just 10 years old. The little boy imagined from this experience that his mother left him specifically, and that could only mean one thing: he is not important, not valuable; there is something wrong with him. As an adult man his sexual experience with women became associated with the positive feedback that he is a valuable person. He put it this way: 'When Vivien makes love to me, I feel valuable. However, when she rejects me, a very dark thought takes over me. I start to feel that there's something wrong with me, because I cannot be desired, I cannot be wanted.' After they both realised what sex represented for Ben, I asked Vivien to reinforce Ben in his value without having to have sex with him against her will. After a few failed attempts, she constructed a very heartfelt message: 'Ben, it has never occurred to me that you wouldn't be valuable to me. I choose you, because for me you are The Man. I long for you, I love you and I want you, but I can't get myself to have sex when our daughter is sick or when I have to close the accounting on time. I'm happy to make love to you next weekend, but please accept for now that I'll just hug you and then I have to go and take care of our little girl.' After these words, Ben had tears in his eyes and said he felt better than he ever used to after lovemaking.

As people who love each other, we are not obliged to be always sexually available to each other . . . but we need to be emotionally available to our partner. And couples in better emotional health learn what is behind sex, and try to respond to that deeper need without feeling compelled to have sex even when they don't feel like it.

> **As people who love each other, we are not obliged to be always sexually available to each other . . . but we need to be emotionally available to our partner.**

There is a difference between sex and sex

If you go into a bookshop, you'll probably find writings about sex on two different shelves. You will find technical descriptions on one of these shelves. There will be pictures of male and female genitals in it, you'll find long lists of sexual dysfunctions, and you'll find detailed know-how descriptions about where to caress, what to lick, where to lubricate and how much lubricant to apply, with the promise that magical sex should follow as a result. On the other shelf you will find relationship books that focus more on communication, conflict management and similar things, and as a subchapter of a subchapter they also contain traces of sex because the author has written about sex in some other book recently. In this subsection, I will try to bring the two shelves a little closer together.

When the word 'sex' is heard, for many people the first thing that comes to mind is what the Gottman couple prefer to call 'impersonal sex': 'Many people clearly enjoy, and perhaps even prefer, what we call "impersonal sex" over "personal sex". Impersonal sex is not necessarily about a particular person. Instead it's about a more detached aspect of sexuality – perhaps a fantasy, a perfect body part, or an exciting sexual encounter with a total stranger. Unlike personal sex, impersonal sex does not involve knowing or emotionally connecting with the person you're having sex with.'[66]

Impersonal sex is more about size, performance, fantasies, and less about personal encounters, intimacy, and trust. The great research endeavour launched in the 1950s put sexuality into the spotlight, but, unfortunately, it also emptied sexuality from its person-centred focus by prioritising measurable things. The most famous example of this research orientation is that of William Masters and Virginia Johnson, to whom we owe a great deal. In the TV series *Masters of Sex*, we can follow the story of the research, one of the highlights of which is that Masters' wife fulminates at her husband: 'You're in that examining room night after night, watching people have sex. "Human sexual response," you call it, but there is no humanity in it. It is important work, but it's not life. It's physiology, it's numbers. Nothing that truly matters in this world can be measured like that. The purpose of sex is not orgasm. It is giving life. This is life; this is love. And without it you're just a man, lost in space, calling out, hoping to hear something back.'

> **Impersonal sex is more about size, performance, fantasies, and less about personal encounters, intimacy, and trust.**

Personal sex is nourished by three important prerequisites: romance (which is a mutual agreement between two people that they see each other as special, unique, and irreplaceable, and they would express this in deeds and nourish it in their thoughts), passion (which means consciously nourishing the almost obsessive interest in, curiosity about, desire for, and attraction to their partner, both physically and emotionally) and trust (a deep belief that our partner is on our side and takes our interests into account, even if we don't agree on everything at the moment).

This is where the issue of emotional responsiveness and secure emotional attachment comes into play again. As Sue Johnson puts it, 'In fact, secure bonding and fully satisfying sexuality go hand in hand; they cue off and enhance each other. Emotional connection creates great sex, and great sex creates deeper emotional connection. When partners are emotionally accessible, responsive, and engaged, sex becomes intimate play, a safe adventure.'[67] She also stresses similar ideas as the Gottmans, and presents similar categories between two people who love each other: 'Depending on how comfortable we are with closeness and how safe we feel about needing our loved one, we will have different goals in bed. Accordingly, I have distinguished three types of sex: Isolated Sex, Consolation Sex and Synchronised Sex.'[68]

By 'isolated sex' she means the same as what I described before as 'impersonal'. A deeper connection isn't the goal in this case: rather, the reduction of tension and the pleasure of experiencing orgasm. This type of sex does not focus on valuing the other person, but rather objectifies and uses the person, so it has a toxic effect on marriage in the long run. It is also more characteristic of men than women. Experiencing sex can be exciting in this form as well; but, without a deeper emotional charge, the passion is short-lived. Technical variety is used as an attempt to avoid boredom, so in this type of sex there is a compulsion towards increasingly bolder, more extreme, sometimes bizarre techniques. And this can distort personality in the long run.

> Emotional connection creates great sex, and great sex creates deeper emotional connection.

The basic driver of consolation sex is anxiety *(am I acceptable, am I lovable, am I important to you, am I desirable?)*. Sex in this case is a means of countering some deeper anxiety, and is not primarily a celebration of union with one another, or a celebration of love. This kind of sexual urge appeared in the history of Ann and Gabriel and Ben and Vivien a few pages ago. What seems to bring relief at first can easily become counterproductive in the long run. If the couple use physical intimacy merely to overcome anxiety, this can easily lead to the couple drifting further and further apart.

Synchronised sex is a personal sexual encounter in the fullest sense. It has romance, passion, and trust. Emotional openness, emotional responsiveness, a gentle touch, and erotic discovery culminate in this experience. It's full of playfulness, and it's all about the partners owning their vulnerability because of their mutual trust. The partners express their desires towards each other openly and honestly, and they are happy to fulfil each other's desires. With the help of the mirror neurons in their brains, they detect each other's feelings; they become synchronised, as an iPhone and an iPad become synchronised. The application I downloaded to one of them will also appear on the other, and even the search history of one of the devices can be found on the other. Two people who get in sync with each other show each other their most complete reality without being afraid of injury, because they trust each other. This is the real depth of a relationship; this is the most complete and undisguised encounter between two individuals! This is what makes lovemaking different from mere sex.

This is the real depth of a relationship; this is the most complete and undisguised encounter between two individuals! This is what makes lovemaking different from mere sex.

Personal responsibility

Whichever category you may fall into – whether you have the bigger sexual appetite in the relationship, or you have less, whether stress boosts your libido or reduces it, whether you have grown up with healthy sexual ideas or inherited a distorted idea of sexuality – your sex life is yours, it belongs to you only, and it also has a decisive influence on another person's life, happiness, and quality of life. Therefore, you have to take responsibility for it! Only you can work on your sexuality! This task cannot be transferred: it cannot be delegated to someone else.

Michele Weiner-Davis, founder of the Divorce Busting movement, who wrote a bestseller about sex-starved marriages, writes: 'Human beings are incredibly complex. Although biology undoubtedly influences our sexuality, it is but one among many other factors. When people decide to become sexual, they do so for a variety of reasons besides seeking sexual gratification. They become sexual to feel close emotionally during and/or after sex, to enhance intimacy in general, to please one's partner, to relax, to feel "sexual" or attractive, to express attraction, to reconcile, to procreate, and so on. If you've been thinking that the only good reason to make love or be physical with your spouse is if you feel turned on sexually, think again.'[69]

The story of Bianca and Nathan is a beautiful example of this. The uncertainties surrounding Nathan's work caused him a huge amount of stress. Revenues dropped, ongoing projects stopped, and new customers withdrew. For him, sex had always been the safe zone where he could recharge, and after they had been together he could always look more deeply into his soul and explain to Bianca what was going on in him. He resorted again to the well-established method and initiated sex – however, he felt that Bianca did not respond to his signals with the same passion. As a result, he became insecure and began to back out of the situation. Bianca asked him why he had been slowing down. The dialogue that followed proves a deep connection, understanding and sophistication in their relationship. Nathan said, 'I feel like this isn't as important to you right now as it is to me, so I stopped because I don't want to force something on you that you don't want. I want to love you, and not use you.' Bianca replied, 'It's true that I'm not in such a horny mood right now, but I know it means a lot to you, so I'm happy to go along. I want to give you this present. I hope you don't want to reject my gift, do you? If I didn't offer this, I would feel that you're using me, but if I'm the one who gives it and you're happy for it, I feel that you love me.' His wife's kindness felt really good to Nathan, and he

> 'I stopped because I don't want to force something on you that you don't want. I want to love you, and not use you.'

emotionally replied, 'I can't even find the words to express how much it means to me that I keep receiving gifts from the biggest present of my life. I wouldn't dare to reject such a gift. Thank you!' After this short dialogue, they made passionate love in which they both experienced a more intense orgasm than ever before.

After this short dialogue, they made passionate love in which they both experienced a more intense orgasm than ever before.

They understood the essence of real giving. 'Real giving is when you give to your spouse not what you want or need, but that which your spouse wants and needs. Plus – and this part is important – you don't really have to fully understand why your spouse feels the way s/he does. You don't have to agree with it. You just have to do it. That's what real giving is all about.'[70]

If by any chance, while reading this chapter, you got the feeling that the basic sexual rule of a good marriage and a storm-proof love is to unreservedly serve your partner's sexual needs in everything, whether you want to or not, then I want to reassure you: you don't have to. No way! It is OK to ask each other for sex, and even to have some expectations towards each other regarding this, as Paul suggests in 1 Corinthians 7:3-5. However, Paul was not suggesting we should demand sex, and we cannot misuse Scripture to abuse each other. Deep intimacy and a good sexual relationship are not about letting ourselves be objectified and letting the other take advantage. If you rethink the story of Bianca and Nathan and imagine these two people in front of you, you will realise that they simply do not fit into an exploitative relationship! These two people would never do anything like that to each other, because they respect each other very much and they have much deeper bonds. Our relationship will be storm-proof if we take responsibility for our sexuality ourselves and we work on ourselves. We examine our instinctive reactions and try to trace what previous experiences they may feed on (even as far back as our infancy). Then we try to redefine who we want to be as human beings who are blessed with sexuality. And then, in a long series of deep and honest conversations, we get to know each other and tune into each other's sexuality so we can fill each other's emotional tanks in a playful, creative, and passionate way – sometimes even in bed.

59 John Gottman, Julie Schwartz Gottman, *The Man's Guide to Women*, p. 12
60 Compare: Guy Bodenmann, David Atkins, Marcel Schaer, Valérie Poffet: 'The Association Between Daily Stress and Sexual Activity', in: *Journal of Family Psychology*, 2010/24, pp. 271-279
61 Brittany Wong, 'Does Sex Really Boost Your Immune System?' – source: *https://www.huffpost.com* (accessed: 14/9/2020)
62 Hui Liu, Linda Waite, Shannon Shen, Donna Wang, 'Is Sex Good for Your Health? A National Study on Partnered Sexuality and Cardiovascular Risk Among Older Men and Women', in: *Journal of Health and Social Behaviour*, 2016/57, pp. 276-296
63 Source: *https://nationalpost.com/news/world/porn-sites-free-viewing-offer-during-covid-19-pandemic-renews-accusations-of-exploitation* (accessed: 22/9/2020)
64 John Gottman, Nan Silver, *What Makes Love Last?* (New York: Simon and Schuster, 2012), Kindle edition
65 Peter Rutter, *Sex in the Forbidden Zone* (New York: Fawcett Crest, 1989), pp. 62-63.
66 John Gottman, Julie Schwartz Gottman, *Gott Sex? The Art and Science of Lovemaking* (Seattle: The Gottman Institute, 2013), p. 9
67 Sue Johnson, *Hold Me Tight!* Kindle edition
68 Ibid.
69 Michele Weiner-Davis, *The Sex-starved Marriage: Boosting Your Marriage Libido* (New York: Simon & Schuster, 2003), p. 31
70 Michele Weiner-Davis, *The Sex-starved Marriage*, pp. 35, 36

STORM-PROOF LOVE

Exercises

A Sexual Guide About Me

Write a sexual guidebook about yourself to your partner. Touch on details like: 'What makes you emotionally and physically open?' 'How can you involve me the best?' 'What do I like best about foreplay, and how do you pamper me?' 'How long should the act last?' 'In what position should it happen?' 'What should happen after the act?'

Personal sex

In this exercise, you will have the opportunity to think about what personal/synchronised sex and what impersonal/isolated or consolation sex experiences you have had over the past six months.

Personal/synchronised sex for me is when:

In order to have personal/synchronised sex, I need:

In the last six months, I can recall the following personal/ synchronised sexual encounters with you:

Personal/synchronised sex has the following effects on our relationship:

Impersonal (isolated or consolation sex) happens between us when:

These are my feelings concerning these sexual events:

STORM-PROOF LOVE

I feel impersonal sex has the following effects on our relationship:

_____

_____

I ask you the following concerning our sexuality: _____

_____

_____

Rejection as an intimate experience

In this exercise, first answer the following three questions about yourself; then, together with your partner, formulate sentences on how best to decline each other's sexual advances while responding positively to each other's deeper need, knowing each other's intimacy drives.

1. What do you really want when you want sex?

_____

_____

2. What do you actually protest when you seemingly refuse sex?

_____

_____

4. How can you differently respond to these underlying needs without ruining your sex life?

_____

_____

'To Reproduce In Captivity'
– Sex and Tenderness Under Pressure

Situation 1: The husband takes the initiative, but the wife doesn't feel like having sex. How do you turn down sex while responding to a deeper need?

_____

_____

_____

_____

_____

_____

Situation 2: The wife takes the initiative, but the husband doesn't feel like having sex. How do you turn down sex while responding to a deeper need?

_____

_____

_____

_____

_____

_____

STORM-PROOF LOVE

The Two of Us and Money

After eighteen years, I stood on the bridge together with Dóra. On the right bank of the creek is the playground where our son used to play in the afternoons, and on the left are the university buildings where we spent three wonderful years of our lives. I thought it was impossible to lift the solemn moment higher, but then my wife had a surprise. She put her arm even tighter around me and whispered into my ear, 'Thank you for keeping your promise.'

My romantic emotions were replaced with zigzagging thoughts in a split second. *What is she thinking of? What did I promise?* Her choice of words and their accented pronunciation indicated that the whole issue was serious, indeed. Dóra sensed my confusion. 'Can't you remember?' she said, hurrying to my aid. 'We stood here the same way when you promised we would never be a deprived family again. And you kept your promise.'

> 'We stood here the same way when you promised we would never be a deprived family again. And you kept your promise.'

These short sentences evoked a whole host of not-so-pleasant memories in me. They reminded me how hard I'd had to work to be able to pay the tuition for the university, to be able to provide for my family, and to secure our housing. Some of our quarrels flashed through my mind – the stress of not having enough money had drained our strength so much that we hurled hurtful and harmful words at each other, which made us feel even worse. Then, travelling further back in time, I remembered my memories of being a 9-year-old child in Vojvodina: how my mum scolded me for spreading the sour cream so thickly on the bread that none would be left for my siblings; how many times I had to cycle twelve kilometres on a dilapidated bike to school because my parents didn't have the money to buy a bus ticket; and how we experienced such hyperinflation during the Balkan War that my dad's salary had to be converted to some other currency immediately upon receipt, because a few hours later it would have been worth only half a loaf of bread.

These experiences left deep scars in me. Deprivation was part of where I came from... but I hated living in that state, and decided that it couldn't be part of where I was going. I wanted to show my wife that our destiny was not set in stone, and yes, we could change it. We do not have an obligation to our ancestors to pass on the same bad inheritance we received from them, but we owe it to our children to pass on a better future. I will go further: by overwriting and correcting old patterns, we rehabilitate our ancestors and endow their suffering with a new meaning. All of this was included in that one sentence: 'Thank you for keeping your promise.'

We both started from poor families; and, if we had based our behaviour on the patterns we had received, we had every reason not to make our lives a success financially: but we decided to take a different path. We decided to eradicate the patterns and beliefs that had shackled our families for generations; we decided that we would handle our finances with brutal honesty and transparency; and we decided we would not allow them to stand between us. Instead of letting finances become a source of conflict, we wanted to make finances a resource in our lives. Money cannot be our ally against each other: rather, the two of us are allies in taming money and making it our servant.

> **Money cannot be our ally against each other: rather, the two of us are allies in taming money and making it our servant.**

Life introduced me to many families whose situation was quite different.

Trapped in false beliefs

I have repeatedly emphasised the patterns that parents inadvertently pass on to their children. There are also plenty of such patterns in money management. In many families, rash sentences are uttered daily, which turn into axioms and belief systems in the children, which are then followed as unquestionable truth in adulthood. Because these are never subject to critical review, they can further influence their decisions and their relationship to money undetected. Eventually they will also make comments in front of their children, who, because their parents have said it, will accept it without reservation and embrace it. And this is how one generation after the other is coached to pass on dysfunctional patterns as a dreaded secret to their children.

If all this seems familiar from your own family, stop for a moment, and think about what beliefs form your relationship to money! My own life is evidence that there are transferred beliefs, but I have changed, and have also assisted the process in many other people's lives: change is indeed possible. To succeed, however, you need to know what type of programme your mind is running repeatedly when it comes to money.

'Although we have power over what we believe, what we believe holds real power over us – power to heal and power to destroy,' said Timothy R. Jennings, an American psychiatrist, concerning thoughts, beliefs, and oft-heard or repeated 'truths'.[71] I deeply agree with him, and I think it is perfectly applicable to our present consideration as well. If our suppositions or beliefs have such an impact on our lives, it's time to make a big clean-up of the ideas and principles that secretly influence our financial decisions.

Do you still remember what I wrote about 'laziness' of the brain, driving a car, and automation in conflict management? The same is true for our money management. The brain stores our 'truths' about money and examines every new situation through the filter of this net of beliefs, because it wants to speed up the process to leave as much energy as possible for our next activities; so it quickly comes to a decision that will affect us in a quantifiable way, and this process will reaffirm our belief system. According to the Australian economist Julie Ann Cairns, it is crucial to changing our financial situation that we raise awareness of our beliefs about money, because as long as these unconsciously guide us, no matter how much economic knowledge we gain, our beliefs will sabotage our decisions. We can

> **The brain stores our 'truths' about money and examines every new situation through the filter of this net of beliefs.**

expect real change if we replace sabotaging beliefs with well-functioning, forward-looking beliefs that work together to create our new 'abundance programme'.[72] After proper practice, our brains will use this abundance programme for our financial decisions, so – perhaps for the first time in our lives – our beliefs work for us, not against us.

> We can expect real change if we replace sabotaging beliefs with well-functioning, forward-looking beliefs.

Inspired by Cairns, I myself have examined the statements I heard countless times at home that also determined my relationship to money in the first half of my life. Then I began to critically consider whether these beliefs were good or not, worthy of retention or not. Eventually, I overwrote them with working, more truthful beliefs, and consciously reminded myself of these in my financial decisions so as not to accidentally turn on the old programme.

I stress, these are the myths of my family! Why I share them with you is to encourage you by my example to confront your own myths.

1. 'There is no financial opportunity where I live.'

Our family has a long tradition of looking for prosperity abroad, because it is an established fact that 'there is no money in Hungary'. My grandparents, aunt, uncle, parents, brother, and sister all lived in other countries for longer or shorter periods to make savings in order to have an easier life after returning home. Of course, because 'there is no money in Hungary', the amount earned abroad sooner or later would run out, leaving the family members with two options: to go abroad again, or to stay home. Contrary to this view, I see that there are very elegant and expensive houses in Hungary as well; very expensive cars also travel on Hungarian roads; and people find a way to prosper here as well. It seems that there is money where I live, only we have not yet found a way to earn it. Therefore, the responsibility is not outside of us (we live in the wrong place), but inside us (we need to become better at business).

STORM-PROOF LOVE

I heard the story at a marketing presentation of a bankrupt bank manager who was walking with his little son, who unexpectedly put the question to him, 'Dad, are you a millionaire?' The question hit a sore spot in the banker, but he didn't want to dump his own difficulties on his child, so he decided to get out of the situation quickly with a short answer: 'Yes, my boy. I am a millionaire.' But the boy continued to ask, 'So where are your millions?' The father realised that this conversation could no longer be continued with superficial answers, so, after some contemplation, he said, 'At this moment my millions are in the bank accounts of other people.' The banker later recalled this conversation as one of the great turning points of his financial philosophy. His grief over his bad situation turned into a conscious search for opportunities. Aversion to responsibility turned at that moment into assumption of responsibility.

> **The banker later recalled this conversation as one of the great turning points of his financial philosophy.**

2. 'Time is money'

What an easier life my poor dad and grandfather could have had if only this financial myth had escaped our family. They spent their entire active lives converting their working hours into money. 'If I can earn X forints in one hour, and I need 100 times X forints, I have to work 100 hours.' As a result, they were both lean, muscular, strong men (my grandfather is no longer with us, but my dad is still alive, thanks to God) who had big biceps with veins running on the surface. But, at the same time, they had to deal with a lot of pain. Their shoulders, arms, and joints sustained severe injuries through many decades of hard work.

A lot of people live in the captivity of this myth and exchange their time for money all their lives. However, we can also organise our work in such a way, for example, that the effect of our work is increased. This is called efficiency multiplication, or economy of scale. The baker could bake loaves one by one, but, with proper planning and good organisational skills, he can bake one hundred loaves of bread at the same time. In one case, he gets one loaf with one trip to the oven; in the other, he gets a hundred loaves. So the key is not to work more, but to better organise our work. We shouldn't simply aim to work more, but to work better! There are those who go so far in this efficiency optimisation that they can make a good living from working up to four hours a week, while freeing up a lot of time for activities and relationships that are important to them.[73]

3. 'You can't get rich from honest work'

Have you heard the term 'honest poverty'? The idea it conveys is very dangerous. It is as dangerous as the 'chubby but at least faithful' life principle, as we will see later. The prisoners of this myth absolve themselves of a higher level of responsibility for their material life by affixing moral labels to people. According to them, wealthy people could only get to where they are now by cheating, and the poor were obviously decent, as they did not fall victim to the lure of wealth and did not take crooked paths to obtain it.

I had especially many problems with this particular idea. I believed this myth with my mind, but I longed for more in my feelings. I tried to resolve the contradiction between the two by watching people living a higher-than-average standard of life in my surroundings and using a magnifying glass to find their faults. I am now very ashamed of this, but emotional health also means owning our mistakes. When one of them became seriously

> I tried to resolve the contradiction between the two by watching people living a higher-than-average standard of life in my surroundings and using a magnifying glass to find their faults.

ill, I felt my own logic justified: since he had sacrificed his health for money, I would rather remain poor, but at least healthy. Another got into trouble with the tax authorities, which once again justified me, as I would rather be poor but law-abiding. The marriage of the third one ended in divorce . . .

STORM-PROOF LOVE

At one point, however, my theory failed. I met someone – who has since become a close friend of our family – who had built up a serious company from scratch. She lives in above-average financial conditions, she is a law-abiding, honest person, she is healthy, she is exemplary in her marriage and family life, and, as if that weren't enough, she donates a lot for good causes and is a really good person. I could almost feel the long-held and maintained structure cracking in my mind. It didn't matter how closely I examined this person: there was nothing foul to be found. I had to admit, my paradigm was wrong! Just because there are those who get their wealth in a crooked way doesn't mean I can arrive at the conclusion that all wealthy people are immoral, nor that all poor people are moral.

4. 'Money won't buy you happiness.'

I'm skating on thin ice with this one. Obviously, we won't be happy just because we have money, but the constant worry, nervousness, and tension over the lack of money can make us downright unhappy and even (physically and mentally) ill. I've talked to a lot of bitter poor people before – as well as to a lot of wealthy people with anxiety and depression . . . so we need to make the picture more nuanced. Money alone can't really make you happy, but it can contribute to a more balanced, healthier, and calmer life, and this can contribute to our happiness. If we look at the financial differences between couples who went through lockdown successfully and those who went through it less successfully, it certainly turns out that it doesn't hurt a happy relationship if the couple also have some money.

It doesn't hurt a happy relationship if the couple also have some money.

The effect of financial satisfaction on a relationship

In our research, we asked several questions about the financial situation of the respondents. These questions were borrowed from the US Financial Consumer Protection Bureau's Financial Satisfaction Survey. Here, again, the results show that there are significant differences between couples that can grow in a storm and those that suffer from a storm:

Statement	Developing couples	Declining couples
I could handle a major unexpected expense.	62%	47%
I am securing my financial future.	74%	50%
Because of my money situation, I feel like I will never have the things I want in life.	12%	25%
I can enjoy life because of the way I'm managing my money.	72%	42%
I am just getting by financially.	13%	23%
I am concerned that the money I have or will save won't last.	10%	22%
Giving a gift for a wedding, birthday or other occasion would put a strain on my finances for the month.	25%	35%
I have money left over at the end of the month.	81%	74%
I am behind with my finances.	7%	13%
My finances control my life.	22%	34%

It is clear from the comparison that, without exception, respondents who lived in a developing relationship performed better on all points. Thus, a clear correlation can be observed between the stability of the relationship and the financial satisfaction of the parties involved in the relationship. Those who are more satisfied with their financial situation are more likely to live in a better-quality relationship. This is confirmed by David Olson's research, which summarises the responses of 50,000 couples:[74]

Statement	Happy couples	Unhappy couples
We agree on how to spend money.	85%	43%
We are satisfied with our decisions about saving.	67%	29%
Major debts are not a problem.	69%	35%
My partner is not trying to control our finances unilaterally.	74%	43%
Use of credit cards is not a problem for us.	69%	42%

Olson himself notes that the 'poor but happy' myth was busted through the family research. According to him, 'Economic hardship and problems in couple and family relationships are often related. Researchers have found that divorce, marital separation, domestic violence, and the abuse of alcohol and other drugs are more likely among the poor than in any other socioeconomic group. . . . Earning an adequate income and managing money efficiently and effectively are important for couples' and families' well-being. If they have enough money to meet their basic needs, couples and families can turn their attention to enhancing the quality of their lives and their relationships.'[75]

Regularly arguing over money is one of the surest predictors of the threat of divorce.[76] It seems that we can extend the idea of the medieval scholastic, Thomas Aquinas, to marriages as well: a moral life requires a minimum level of material well-being, and a good marriage requires a certain level of financial well-being. This is not to say that the richer someone is, the better their marriage will be. Money is not a substitute for the many efforts that are necessary to grow a relationship or to develop a marriage daily. However, having money helps a lot so that worry doesn't overwhelm your relationship; and, if you learn to manage your resources well, you will simultaneously accumulate a range of relationship skills that will improve the quality of your marriage. On the other hand, many make the mistake of trying to compensate with money for what they do not put into the relationship. However, this attempt will quickly fail. This is also suggested by research which found a direct relationship between the price of an engagement ring, the budget of the wedding, and the likelihood of a divorce.[77] Interestingly, the more expensive the wedding, the more likely it is that the marriage will not be long-lasting.

> **Many make the mistake of trying to compensate with money for what they do not put into the relationship. However, this attempt will quickly fail.**

You cannot survive without savings!

Although there has been an increase of responsibility in our money-management habits in recent years, it remains very important to emphasise the importance of saving. Let me show you an analysis of my own country. Currently, two thirds of the Hungarian population have savings. This sounds good at first, but if we look a little deeper into the pockets, we find cause for concern. Thirty-one percent of the population have savings of less than 300 euros, 37% have an amount between 300 and 3,000 Euros, and 33% have more than 3,000 Euros. In the UK, nearly a fifth of all adults have less than £100 in savings, and the number of people unable to save at all doubled between 2019 and 2021.[78]

The basic rule is that every financial unit should have a reserve equal to at least three – preferably six – months of operating costs. This means that if the cash flow is blocked tomorrow, the unit would be able to continue to operate for months. Because the family is also an economic unit, it is a necessity that these savings are available for an eventual crisis.

When I talk about this in a lecture, usually someone remarks, 'It's easy for someone to make savings who has enough income to save from.' If the financial security of our family is important to us, let's quickly erase this argument from our heads! No one will take financial responsibility for our family instead of ourselves. In my pastoral ministry, I myself have repeatedly been amazed at the serious sums people have been able to save from an impossibly small income with a disciplined budget. When, for example, we built a new church and community house for our congregation, pensioners with very little income, who made a living by tending to small cattle around their household all their life, donated significant amounts to the project. There are people on very low incomes who are still able to save monthly, and there are people with a high income living in big houses and driving expensive cars who are in debt. Savings do not depend on income, but on the mindset!

I won't write in detail about the practical side of savings here, but I suggest making a family budget plan, which is a great aid to this process. There are many different definitions of a budget, but I like the following one, which seems to encompass them all: a budget means you tell your money where to go, instead of asking at the end of the month where your money has gone.

Savings do not depend on income, but on the mindset!

The importance of saving is particularly emphasised at those stages of life when the family must cope suddenly with much higher costs than usual. Research shows that these periods are the time after the birth of the children, the adolescence of the children, the departure of the young adults, and the retirement period, when the couple have to maintain their normal standard of living with less income.[79] The list shows that particularly money-intensive stages of life develop around life-cycle changes and are often related to children. Of course, there are many different tax and other benefits for having children, but we also need to be prepared for the higher costs involved. Back in 2011, I heard from Professor Mária Kopp in a lecture that raising a child until graduation in Hungary costs the price of a medium-sized family house … and this must be multiplied by the number of children in our family.

In addition to predictable life-cycle changes for everyone, commonly referred to as normative crises, unexpected situations such as accidents, illness, natural disasters, pandemics, job losses, and so on can arise in a matter of seconds that require us to reach deeper into our pockets. Whatever situation we look at, we can't afford to run our budget to zero. Make sure you have a savings plan today, and start consciously putting money aside.

We cannot close this subchapter without talking about 'negative savings' – that is, debt. Today, we do not have the time and patience to wait for many things, and, as a result, too many are still in debt without considering the long-term consequences. One side of the consequences is material in nature, while the other side concerns the relationship. From a financial point of view, of course, we must think through how monthly repayments affect our daily lives. Will we be able to pay even if one of us temporarily loses their job, falls ill, or has less income due to some other circumstance? Is there any other way besides credit to get the thing you crave for? As for myself, I try to avoid any commitment in which I become dependent on others, in which others can decide over me, over my home, or over other properties. Usually, the other party is not driven by a selfless charitable intent to lend me the money, but is driven purely by business interests; and, when interests clash, it can easily lead to harm and pain.

> Today, we do not have the time and patience to wait for many things, and, as a result, too many are still in debt without considering the long-term consequences.

STORM-PROOF LOVE

In addition, there is also a long list of relationship consequences. In a sense, taking out a loan is like having a child. Just as it is proper to have children in a committed, well-functioning, stable marriage, so it is proper to take up a long-term financial commitment if there are similar basic conditions, because if the relationship results in a break-up, the divorced will face a series of new questions: whose decision was it to take out the loan? Who carries the consequences of this decision? In what proportion is the consequence shared? Is it possible to end the relationship while still having a common obligation? Who stays in the home and who moves out? How does the remaining party compensate the one who needs to move out? I know this seems drastic wording, but let me tell you, a crisis can bring a lot out of us that we did not know before about ourselves, so it is worth it to mitigate the risks: and this is the easiest at the beginning of the story.

> **If the relationship results in a break-up, the divorced will face a series of new questions: whose decision was it to take out the loan?**

Separate or common budget?

A young couple still before their wedding sat in front of me, Zoey and Aaron. I was asked to help them prepare for marriage and review the results of the Couple's Check-up Inventory together. I'm always amazed when a couple are so conscious that they're looking for the best way to start their marriage right from the start, so of course I was happy to support them. When we got to the family budget, I asked them:

'Tell me, have you talked about how you're going to handle your money when you're married?'

A mischievous smile appeared on Aaron's face, as if eager to answer:

'Yes, we have a clear plan for that. Since I have an accounting degree anyway and I work in this profession, it's obvious that I'll manage the money. And because I understand it better, I will make the decisions, and Zoey agrees with this.

The Two of Us and Money

I looked at Zoey and saw that she was smiling approvingly, proving that they indeed had already talked and come to this agreement, but behind her smile I sensed some uncertainty as well. As she was looking at me, she kept biting her lips as if she wanted to say something but would rather not say anything to avoid getting into trouble. I asked Aaron to look at his bride and tell me what he saw.

'Well, she is biting her lips just like when we are arguing.'

Then I asked Zoey what that something was that she was so eager to say but had been trying her best to hold back. She replied:

'It's true that we agreed on this, but I have reservations about it. So far, I've always had to ask my dad for money if I wanted to buy something, and I hoped that we'd be equal in the marriage, and we would decide everything together. But now I'm afraid it will continue to be the same, only from now on I must beg you, not my dad.'

> But behind her smile I sensed some uncertainty as well. As she was looking at me, she kept biting her lips.

Zoey could not have formulated the danger of their plan more expertly! If she can't feel equal in her marriage and has to beg her husband for everything, a subordinate relationship will emerge very soon, and this will start to adversely affect her self-esteem as well as their intimacy. True intimacy is created between two people of equal rank: but if the wife sees her husband as a father figure, rather than as an equal partner, it will trigger hidden taboos that were coded into her. We're not going to bed with our father! We don't get into an intimate situation with our daughter! Her words led us to renegotiate the issue and find a solution in which their equality was better expressed and in which Zoey also feels that she has an influence on the financial side of their relationship.

After the story, let's look at what research has to say on this topic. What can you do to do the best for your marriage? Shall you manage your money together or separately? There are three types of money-management methods in the family: the separate accounts (everyone manages their own income, but they agree how to cover the shared costs); the partly shared account (some of their income is put into a shared account to cover shared expenses, and the rest is independently owned by the parties and spent as they like); and the joint account (all income arrives into one account and is then used to cover the expenses, and individual allowances are also redistributed by mutual agreement from there). According to a study by the Finance Faculty at the University of California, the joint account method has the best effect on relationship satisfaction and relationship durability. The result can be summarised in the following table:[80]

Method of money management	Relationship satisfaction (1-7)	Divorce (after less than 10 years)
Joint account	6.10	24%
Partly shared account	5.82	26%
Separate accounts	5.46	30%

According to the study, joint money management also has a beneficial effect on the development of a couple's 'we' consciousness: they feel more reciprocal in the relationship, and they feel more equal than couples following the other two ways of money management. It is also clear from the table that they are more satisfied with their relationship and are less likely to divorce than the followers of the partially shared or separate accounts. 'Our findings are not simply the result of more satisfied couples being more likely to join their accounts. Rather, these results demonstrate that the method of account management can also influence relationship quality.'[81]

The desirable side effect of a joint account is that the couple must constantly agree with each other on finances, and as a result their values get aligned, they gain more practice in joint planning and decision-making, a more stable balance of power evolves between them, more trust builds in each other, and they both feel they can influence their relationship.

Of course, there are also special situations when it needs to be considered whether to get into joint money management. An example for this is a relationship of less than one year in which the parties are not committed to each other. But caution needs to be exercised if the partner is abusive. In these cases, always have private savings in case you must flee suddenly. Caution also needs to be practised if one partner has an addiction, because addiction can lead to irrational decisions, so it's important not to have all the resources of the family in one place. Another important reason can be psychological illness, since the affected person is not always in control of his or her actions and decisions, and therefore might act irresponsibly, to the detriment of the whole family.

---

[71] Timothy R. Jennings, *The God-shaped Brain: How Changing Your View of God Transforms Your Life* (Downers Grove: InterVarsity Press, 2017)
[72] Julie Ann Cairns, *The Abundance Code: How to Bust the 7 Money Myths for a Rich Life Now* (Hay House, 2015), Kindle edition
[73] Compare: Timothy Ferriss, *The 4-Hour Work Week* (Ebury Publishing, 2011)
[74] David H. Olson, Amy Olson-Sigg, Peter J. Larson, *The Couple Checkup: Find Your Relationship Strengths* (Nashville: Thomas Nelson, 2008), pp. 90-91
[75] David H. Olson, John DeFrain, *Marriages & Families: Intimacy, Diversity and Strengths* (Boston: McGraw Hill, 2006), p. 215
[76] Jeffrey Dew, Sonya Britt, Sandra Huston: 'Examining the Relationship Between Financial Issues and Divorce', in: *Family Relations*, 2012/61, pp. 615-628
[77] Andrew Francis-Tan, Hugo M. Mialon, ' "A Diamond is Forever" and Other Fairy Tales: The Relationship Between Wedding Expenses and Marriage Duration', *https://ssrn.com/abstract=2501480* (accessed: 28/8/2020)
[78] Sources: *https://forbes.hu/penz/a-magyarok-ketharmada-rendelkezik-megtakaritassal-de-a-kiszamithatosag-fontosabb-mint-a-magas-hozam/* (accessed: 26/08/2020) and *https://www.ybs.co.uk/media-centre/savings-crisis/index.html* (accessed: 13/10/2021)
[79] Olson, DeFrain, *Marriages & Families*, p. 217
[80] J. Gladstone, E. N. Garbinsky, C. Mogilner, 'Pooling Finances and Relationship Satisfaction', *https://www.anderson.ucla.edu/faculty-and-research/anderson-review/joint-bank-account* (accessed: 27/8/2020)
[81] Ibid.

STORM-PROOF LOVE

Exercises

Our family money myths

At the beginning of the chapter, I presented how our beliefs about money affect our thinking, decisions, and ultimately our financial situation. Now it is your turn. Review the money myths circulating in your family, and make them the subject of critical scrutiny!

Family myths about money:

_____

_____

_____

_____

_____

_____

Have these beliefs helped or hindered you in your life so far? (Justify your answer!)

_____

_____

_____

_____

_____

_____

_____

What new beliefs would you like to replace them with, something you are happy to pass on to your own children?

_____

_____

_____

_____

_____

_____

_____

Savings plan

It would be good if, like all economic units, the family had financial reserves equal to at least three months' operating costs.

1. How much does it cost to maintain your family in a month? List all expenses, and be as detailed as you can!

_____

_____

_____

_____

_____

_____

2. How long could you continue to live at the same standard from your current reserves if suddenly you had no income?

_____

3. What steps do you need to take together to have three months' worth of operating costs?

_____

_____

_____

_____

_____

4. What are your short-, medium- and long-term financial goals?

_____

_____

_____

_____

_____

Let's make good decisions!

The husband's aunt sends a voucher worth £1,000. The voucher can be redeemed at any webshop, but only today. What you do not use from the amount today will be invalid tomorrow.

1. Search various webshops and then spend (of course, only pretending to buy) the full imaginary amount! List what you have spent the money on:

_____

_____

_____

2. How did you make this decision? Whose vote was decisive for each product?

3. Did you feel equal in your decision-making?

4. Did it matter whose relative you got the money from?

5. What would you do differently next time, if the situation were to happen for real?

STORM-PROOF LOVE

Organised Living Space and Personal Care

During the lockdown, I moved my couple's therapy practice to the online space, gaining unprecedented insight into the inner world of the couples, into their physical space where they lived their lives daily. Their surroundings often revealed much more than their well-dressed and well-groomed appearance in my office.

The case of Leslie and Judy is a good example of this phenomenon. Imagine a typical middle-class couple with three children, both employed. They don't live an extravagant life, but they have everything they need. They are loyal to each other, committed to their family, and do their best for their children. Yet they are unhappy. Leslie described their lives as follows: 'The years go by, but we are stuck in the same place.'

So far, I hadn't realised anything special about them; they had always appeared smartly dressed and clean. Now, however, I could observe them in their 'natural habitat'. This encounter put them in a whole new light. Judy was sitting in front of the screen in a shabby T-shirt with uncombed hair, and Leslie was wearing a crinkled undershirt and had at least four-day-old stubble. Suddenly I thought to myself, 'All we need now is for him to stand up and reveal that he has only underpants and no trousers.' Unfortunately, my suspicion was later confirmed! Really! Imagine, he really sat down for a couple's therapy session in a vest and a pair of pants. Then I observed the room they were sitting in. Behind them was an unmade double bed (we talked at three in the afternoon!), the clothes in the armchair waited to be ironed in a tall tower, and there was no lampshade on the ceiling, only two wires and a naked light bulb. When asked, I was told this was the normal condition in their home. They felt a little uncomfortable that they couldn't receive guests, but they're used to it, and the kids felt good about it, too. They moved into their house five years ago, and, as they put it, they occupied their home from room to room, so there was no lamp in the bedroom yet.

I decided to incorporate my observations into the therapeutic process and set off in a whole new direction. These two people must first learn to take their lives back into their own hands, and only then can it be possible to explore deeper emotions and deal with conflict more effectively. First, I asked them to tell each other how it felt for each of them to see the other one in such a state. It turned out that they were both disturbed by the sight, but this was never mentioned, because then they would have had to change themselves, too. Then we agreed that they would regain control of their bodies, and next time they would be as well-groomed and pretty as if we met in person in my office. And they would pay attention to this not only on the days when we have a therapy session, but every day of the week, for themselves and for each other.

Then came the more difficult task. They had to sort out that mess!

Then came the more difficult task. They had to sort out that mess! We agreed they would take advantage of the potential of the lockdown, when they could spend a lot of time at home and when the kids had more time as well, to make a plan to tidy up their home. First, in the morning, everyone could make their bed after getting up, and then, little by little, they would clear the backlog in housework, dividing the tasks among the family members. And one more thing: they couldn't live in an environment similar to a construction site for any more years. They could order lampshades for each room on the internet, and let's have Leslie instal them! As it turned out, Leslie is a very skilful handyman, and the lamp installation proved to be the most successful father-son programme of recent years. And, as the weeks passed, the family slowly regained control of their lives, and the couple also grew closer to each other, which started to show its impact on their intimacy as well.

Of course, this is just one story among many, so let's see what the numbers show! Is there a difference between couples in declining relationships and those in developing ones?

STORM-PROOF LOVE

Statement	Developing couples	Declining couples
During the lockdown, we revised our daily tasks and set a new agenda.	67%	40%
It gave me a sense of security during the lockdown that we had planned our days.	69%	34%
Our days went by during the lockdown.	18%	34%
I paid attention to my appearance; even at home, I was pretty and tidy.	68%	42%
Our home is tidy and clean.	85%	70%
During lockdown we slept in long in the mornings and went to bed late.	32%	32%

As can be seen from the data, in the study – inspired by the story of Leslie, among others – I focused on three areas: agenda, living space and personal hygiene. Let's take a closer look at their significance.

Agenda

Let's go back to Leslie and Judy for a moment. It turned out that the flexibility provided by the home office made it possible for them to sleep in during the mornings, which in turn made it possible for them to regularly watch TV until two at night, which, of course, resulted in not being able to get up on time. Practically their whole day just got wasted. They couldn't pay attention to their work because they were guilty of neglecting their children, and when they were with their children they felt bad for not making any progress in their work. Basically, nothing happened, and the chaos just grew bigger and bigger . . .

Unstructured days and faltering relationships: is there a connection between the two? You bet! In our study, four questions also addressed this topic, and three of them showed significant differences (there was no difference in terms of sleeping time patterns). However, the conclusion is still quite clear: the structuring of time has a measurable effect on the quality of the relationship.

During the lockdown, I watched the statements and survival tips of leading couple's therapists and psychologists, and one thing always came back as if they had just agreed beforehand: set an agenda and stick to it!

I asked many couples how they plan their days. They shared many ideas with me. I got the most detailed description from Attila, who after the first few days realised that they had to completely rethink their relationship to time management in order to survive the lockdown. If they still wanted to be in love after the storm, they had to make decisions and take action during the storm. **Unstructured days and faltering relationships: is there a connection between the two?** They are a couple in their thirties who spent the pandemic at home together. Attila has children from his previous relationship, but he couldn't visit them now, so it was just the two of them, him and Csilla, all the time. To add to their woes, Csilla was sent home on unpaid leave, and Attila would have changed jobs, but could not start working at the new company, so they had to live on their reserves. For many this would be heaven on earth; for others it would be a living hell – to be together from dawn to dusk, every day of the week! When Attila sent me their agenda, he remarked, 'If we hadn't followed an agenda, we would have been lying in bed with severe depression for a long time. Instead, we feel vibrant, ready to act, and happy. This is largely due to our new routine.' Let's see what they did differently compared to their old lives!

'We used to start with coffee every morning, but we barely took a sip; we were already on our mobiles, we were playing games on them, we were reading articles, we gave likes to totally unnecessary stuff. And

STORM-PROOF LOVE

before we went to work we quickly and guiltily hugged each other for one last time, because we felt we had wasted the morning.

'According to our new routine, we used our morning coffee for one thing only: to set our goal for the day, and to rethink the short- and long-term goals as well. It always initiates a brain-stimulating, constructive, mutually supportive conversation between us; it smuggles enthusiasm into our morning that persists throughout the day if we manage to focus on our daily goal. And we do not think of great things.

'It smuggles enthusiasm into our morning that persists throughout the day if we manage to focus on our daily goal.'

For me, for example, all I need to do today is to fix the chaos of the browser tabs open on my phone. Csilla needs to write an outline of a study chapter for the training she enrolled in.

'As a short-term goal, she set out to develop a strategy for more effective note-taking, and I set out to accumulate more knowledge. In the long run, we both want to live out our passions.

'I think we've skilfully shopped: there's at least a month's worth of food in the fridge and in the larder, but the selection isn't large. This made it easier to edit the menu, as we vary the same dishes every week.

'We exercise every morning from 9 to 10. Actually, the training lasts only half an hour, and then we need another 30 minutes to regain consciousness, shower, hug and congratulate each other.

'We study from 10 to 11! This is very important because we want to get out of lockdown smarter than the way we went in. This is a common activity. We choose a topic together; if there is a video about it, we watch it together, and we discuss it together. We're picking from a variety of knowledge bases, but there's also plenty to learn on YouTube in every language.

'We have a "zone time" from 11 to noon. We call it "zone time" when everyone is doing what they would like. For example, I am writing this email to you in this timeslot. Csilla started to do some handicraft.

'At noon I start slicing the vegetables, and by the time I have to stir them over the stove my faithful cook is already there to help. We have *fun times in the kitchen. In addition to eating lunch, we usually watch one episode of our current favourite TV series. This is followed by a siesta. We've heard that our immune system desperately needs a state of rest, so we can afford this luxury between 1pm and 3pm.*

'Then zone time from 3pm to 6pm again. I usually play (PS4), read or study. Csilla writes outlines or notes, makes crafts or studies craft videos.

'We have dinner at 6pm, and call our parents at 7.

'Once we are both happy that our loved ones are well, a mandatory inhalation is introduced. We boil water with a little chamomile tea and inhale alternately for 5-10 minutes; or, while one of us inhales the hot air, the other quietly meditates, concentrating on his own breathing, calming his mind, appreciating her day, rearranging the ranks of his spiritual soldiers. I honestly admit, this is my favourite part of the day, because at such times there is such a peace that no fear can corrode. This is followed by a shower, and we are ready for your 9 o'clock Couple-Minutes Programme.

> **'I honestly admit, this is my favourite part of the day, because at such times there is such a peace that no fear can corrode.'**

'After that we're just watching TV or reading . . . or we play board games.

'In addition to all this, I also have a mandatory routine: on every even date (like today on the 22nd) I check the pantry and the fridge for sorry-looking vegetables, fruits, or foods with tighter expiration dates to be eaten the next day. I don't want to find rotten carrots that have already infected the other vegetables at the bottom of the fridge in two weeks' time.

'These routine tasks are written on a sheet of paper and posted on the door of our wardrobe to always keep them in mind. At the bottom of the list is a detailed "what to do if we catch the virus" appendix, thus preventing unnecessary panic.'

I accept any suggestion you might make that this agenda is a bit exaggerated and feels like the military. I haven't shared Attila's letter so that everyone would follow the same agenda when the apocalypse hits, but because I really like the thinking that lies behind it. This couple recognised that the new situation required new solutions. They thought over what they needed to do to survive the uncertain and unknown period waiting for them. They even decided at the beginning that they wanted to emerge stronger from the crisis. Based on a joint decision, they put together a plan that had enough freedom to implement spontaneous ideas, but also included exercise and conscious attention to eating and learning. This is not to say that they masochistically stopped everything they were happy to do in the past, but they had to accept some constraints in order to maintain balance.

Since ancient times, the community of the table has been a very powerful symbol of belonging together – think of Leonardo da Vinci's painting, 'The Last Supper'.

Attila returned several times in his description to common meals. I also would like to bring this to your attention, whether it is just the two of you or you have a bigger family. Eating together has an incredibly important relationship- and community-building role. It is no coincidence that, since ancient times, the community of the table has been a very powerful symbol of belonging together – think of Leonardo da Vinci's painting, 'The Last Supper'.

In addition to spending time together, eating together also has a number of long-term blessings. Studies at Andrews University in Michigan show that in families that are eating together:[82]

- There is a lower risk of family breakdown,
- Children achieve better learning outcomes,
- There are fewer teenage pregnancies,
- Family members have higher individual resilience,
- Family members eat healthier and more regularly,
- Family members are less prone to obesity,
- Drug abuse is less common,
- Family members have higher self-confidence,
- Family members are less likely to develop depression.

Attila also mentions in his letter that the joint preparation of the food brought them closer together. I heard from a couple living in Sweden that one of the best family team-building exercises they ever completed was a home-delivery food service where no ready-made food could be ordered, only the exact ingredients and the recipe for how to prepare it, which the family then had to prepare together.

So, if you get into a storm and want to get out of it in a better state than you went in, here's the recipe! Together, create a new agenda that guides you through the chaos, helps you focus on the important things, and prevents you from taking up unhealthy and, in the long run, relationship-straining habits.

> Together, create a new agenda that guides you through the chaos.

And, speaking of habits, I can't leave out the relevant lesson from Stephen Covey's ingenious concept either. Examining the habits of highly effective people, Covey concluded that these individuals do their daily tasks and make their decisions in a certain order. The driving force behind their routine is the 'first things first' principle. There are so many events, things to do, activities on a given day. So many people and things compete for our attention that we need serious self-discipline and motivation to feel productive at the end of the day, without having to go to bed with the frustration of not accomplishing anything we wanted to because we went with the flow. Covey suggests a helpful time-management matrix where one axis is urgency and the other is importance, known as the Eisenhower matrix. Rank your daily tasks (and your intrusive, distracting activities) according to the following simple categories:[83]

1. **Place: urgent and important.** This includes all tasks that cannot be postponed and are important to you or others: for example, tasks with deadlines or taking your child to the orthodontist are urgent and important. Start with these!
2. **Place: important but not urgent.** In here belongs the list of how much and for what purpose to transfer money. My promise to my parents that I would go to the tile shop with them to help choose

the style of the new bathroom also ends up here. These have no specific deadlines, but they need to be done. Then why would we procrastinate? If we have finished the tasks with a deadline, let's do these ones too!

3. **Place: not important but urgent.** We deal with this category after the important things are already done. This usually includes activities related to fun, relaxation, and emotions – like the new season of your favourite series released on Netflix. Nothing bad happens if you don't look into it for a week, except your curiosity torturing you a bit. No problem! If you have done all the important things, reward yourself by watching a little . . . but only then!

4. **Place: not urgent and not important.** These are impulses that unnecessarily grab your attention in order to start serving someone else's interests, such as impulse shopping in the shop, an interesting Facebook ad, or a pop-up window on one of the websites. You've been fine without these things so far, but now you imagine (the marketing is working) that you absolutely need this product, experience, event, and so on.

> **The space in which we live our lives can be a source of balance, but it can also be a source of stress.**

It is not the relaxation or the impulse consumption itself that is the problem. The trouble comes when satisfying those impulses becomes the priority, and you no longer have the strength, the time, or the attention to do the really important things. First things first!

Living space

Although spatial psychology is still only an evolving trend among a wide range of psychological trends, several studies have emerged in recent decades that have examined the relationship between living space and state of mind. The space in which we live our lives can be a source of balance, but it can also be a source of stress that, in addition to other negative effects, sucks the last drop of life force out of us. If we lose control of our home, it can cause chronic exhaustion and, in the long run, lead to learnt inertia, which slowly spreads into all areas of our lives. In the end, it is not we who exercise control over our lives, but we are constantly reacting to events and trying to solve those problems in panic where the situation is already very threatening.[84]

The negative effects of messiness were also shown in our study. Eighty-five percent of those in developing relationships said their homes were tidy and clean, compared with 70% in declining relationships. Even if the difference is not as big as in other areas, there is still a detectable difference!

Interestingly, the research also shows a gender difference. There were studies that monitored the stress levels of the subjects throughout the working day and found that men were much more stressed at work than at home, while women experienced the opposite. Women were calmer at work, but they were severely stressed by how many more tasks awaited them at home, and as a result many sought the opportunity for a little overtime to postpone facing a 'second shift' at home. Therefore, it is important – especially in families where both parents work outside the home – to share household responsibilities between husband and wife. Make your home an island of tranquillity and regeneration for both parties.

Eighty-five percent of those in developing relationships said their homes were tidy and clean, compared with 70% in declining relationships.

Pennebaker and colleagues conducted exciting research to assess the effects of the living space. Thirty families were visited and asked to guide the researchers through their homes and introduce them to each room as if their homes were a tourist attraction, and they were the tour guides. The presentation was recorded, followed by various physiological measurements and relationship tests. The result: those who spoke positively, proudly, and happily about their homes as a place of calm, peace and recharge had lower levels of stress hormone than those who attached negative words to their homes, were ashamed of the mess, and did not feel well generally in their living space. The first group were also in better physical condition, more satisfied with their relationship, and tested to be more mentally stable than the second group.[85] The research was repeated several times, with similar results. Order and mess, as well as completeness and incompleteness, were significant factors in whether the 'tour guides' spoke positively or negatively about their homes.

A messy home leads to undisciplined and discursive thinking, which jeopardises the stability of the relationship. Therefore, someone whose life is completely messy (for example, in the web of an addiction) is first taught how to keep their living space clean and tidy, and then they can help to unravel other problems. However, we will learn more about this soon.

Tidying up has tremendous power. Tidying up has tremendous power. When we get into a situation that is uncontrollable for us, it causes anxiety in us. A good practice when losing control is to start controlling what you do have control over. If the waves crash over my head and I feel like I can't see through my commitments and threatening deadlines, I take a deep breath and put my desk in order. This gives me a feeling of power, and I feel that I am no longer a victim of my circumstances, but a controller. I will have the strength to face the tasks and solve them one after the other. And what I don't have power over is easier to accept, because I have reserves and I no longer doubt my abilities. This is why patients with anxiety are also advised to act against their uncontrollable anxiety by controlling their living space – that is, to put their stuff in order.[86] And that's why it's also an important cornerstone of educational materials to prevent addictions in children: keep order around you! An orderly environment results in orderly thinking, and whoever thinks in an orderly manner can resist pressure and temptation.[87]

Personal hygiene

I was just getting ready one night for a Facebook live event when Dóri stepped into the room. She sniffed the air and immediately identified the scent of my favourite body perfume. She asked me with a surprised expression, 'Did you forget you're going to perform in front of a camera? No one will smell the perfume on you.' 'No, my love,' I replied after a short pause; 'I know exactly that the scent will not get through the camera, but I also know that if I feel good, more of my best will be seen through the camera.'

Whether it's just my personal whim that I only feel good in my skin when I'm well-groomed, or whether this is a general human trait, will be told by the numbers. We also asked in the research whether during the lockdown (when only the close family could see it) the respondents paid attention to their appearance, to ensuring they were pretty and well-groomed. There is a difference here as well. More than two thirds (68%) of those in a developing relationship answered yes, while only 42% of those in a declining relationship said the same. It does matter if we feel pretty, pleasant-looking and well-scented, because it will affect our behaviour and aura. Just remember back to your adolescence, how much you worried about what the others would say about your appearance, your clothes. Are we going to be good enough? These thoughts distract us from the conversation, and we won't pay attention to the information given by the other person, so we won't be able to participate in the conversation and will prove that we can only focus on ourselves. The outcome of the data can be easily predicted . . .

> **It does matter if we feel pretty, pleasant-looking and well-scented, because it will affect our behaviour and aura.**

We know from research on assertiveness that our focus of attention and self-confidence are closely related.[88] The confident people direct two thirds of their attention outward and one third inward. In contrast, insecure people turn two thirds of their attention inward and only one third outward to deal with their external situation . . . and that will not be enough for a successful outcome.

So, the exterior is important in influencing how we generally feel and therefore what we do. We can draw interesting conclusions from our study about the results of men in this issue. I said earlier that 68%

of people in developing relationships paid attention to their appearance, even during lockdown. However, if we also look at the proportion of men and women, it turns out that 68% of women and 72% of men in this group said yes to this statement. It suggests that men put an effort into the issue, and this was reflected in the upward trend of their relationship. However, 42% of couples with problems said yes to paying attention to their appearance during lockdown; but, among them, 43% of women responded positively, compared to only 34% of men. The conclusion is that in a developing relationship men are taking care of their appearance, but in declining relationships they aren't. (It cannot be concluded from the data alone whether they don't take care of themselves because their relationship is not developing, or whether their relationship is not developing because they are not taking care of themselves. I personally lean towards the latter interpretation.) So, if you are a man and neglect your appearance, you can expect the quality of your relationship to deteriorate. (Of course, this is also true for women, but the negligence of men seems to be statistically even more significant.)

'People do extreme things in the name of beauty. They invest so many of their resources in beauty and risk so much for it, one would think that lives depended on it.'

Most people like to look good. That is why we are also ready to make sacrifices. Nancy Etcoff sums up well how far we are willing to go: 'People do extreme things in the name of beauty. They invest so many of their resources in beauty and risk so much for it, one would think that lives depended on it. In Brazil there are more Avon ladies than members of the army. In the United States more money is spent on beauty than on education or social services. Tons of makeup – 1,484 tubes of lipstick and 2,055 jars of skin care products – are sold every minute. During famines, Kalahari bushmen in Africa still use animal fats to moisturise their skin, and in 1715 riots broke out in France when the use of flour on the hair of aristocrats led to a food shortage. The hoarding of flour for beauty purposes was only quelled by the French Revolution.'[89]

We want to be pretty at all costs. But why? My personal observations, in turn, confirm that, while we have created a huge cult of beauty, our relationship morals and know-how did not develop at the same pace. Dóri and me were in for a surprise several times as we watched our Facebook acquaintances working resolutely on their tummy muscles week after week. Every night one person posted what exercises he did, what diet he followed, to make even the last little bit of fat disappear. Yes, he has proved that, even over 40, great results can be brought out of our bodies. Surprisingly, after some time he also posted that he had just realised how unhappy he had been so far, but now he had found the love of his life in the person of a lady twenty years younger than him, and he was divorcing his wife.

Or there's the lady, a mum and wife, also in her forties, who was coaxed into sports in her late thirties and now wins races, runs marathons, and is successful in other leisure sports. Her sons are proud of her; friends cite her as a motivating positive example; while her husband calls me sobbing in the middle of the night because he can no longer accept that his wife gets into one-night stands at almost every sporting event she attends.

We want to be beautiful. That's OK. But who do we want to be beautiful for? For our partner, in order to strengthen the bond between the two of us even more? Or are we using our beauty as bait to attract the attention of others, and then to cross boundaries that should never be crossed?[90]

Negative examples should be followed by a positive example. On one occasion I attended a training session lasting several months where men and women were present. Here I witnessed one of the male participants of the group starting to pay attention to one of the ladies. At one break, the man asked a question of her: 'Audrey, do you know what a beautiful woman you are?'

> But who do we want to be beautiful for? For our partner, in order to strengthen the bond between the two of us even more? Or are we using our beauty as bait to attract the attention of others?

STORM-PROOF LOVE

The lady smiled confidently and said, 'Yes, Paul. I know exactly what a beautiful woman I am, because I do a lot to be one. But I reserve my beauty for my husband.'

I felt a deep respect for Audrey for saying this. This is the attitude I wish for everyone who lives in a relationship. Do everything for your beauty within normal limits, but know who it is whom you want to please!

Having talked about the pursuit of beauty, let's now have a look at those who neglect to be beautiful. Compared to the cult of deifying beauty, they represent the other extreme. And, as I mentioned several times, the lockdown showed who had reserves of attention to their appearance, and how much of it; thus, it also brought this hidden attitude to the surface. These people threw in the towel and abandoned all control over their appearance. As I saw on one of the memes on social media while the 'stay at home' message was broadcast on every channel: 'I never thought I would save humanity by eating crisps on my couch while watching TV.' This is not the right attitude either. According to a recent lockdown survey, 22% of those who were at home during the pandemic reported gaining 5 to 11 pounds of weight.[91] The study found that the main causes of obesity were irregular sleep, snacks after dinner, undisciplined overeating, eating as stress relief, and lack of exercise. This also affects the relationship. Numerous studies have addressed the relationship between body weight, relationship satisfaction, and sexual behaviour. These demonstrated that being overweight has a negative effect on self-esteem and impairs relationship satisfaction, and that those who are overweight are less likely to make love and more likely to be dissatisfied with their sex lives.[92]

A balance must be achieved. If you are athletic, pretty, and well-groomed, you shouldn't use your advantage to seduce somebody and be unfaithful to your spouse.

A balance must be achieved. If you are athletic, pretty, and well-groomed, you shouldn't use your advantage to seduce somebody and be unfaithful to your spouse. At the same time, it is also inappropriate for people to absolve themselves of responsibility for their bodies by pointing out the infidelity of many who do look after their bodies. The 'I may be chubby but at least I'm loyal' argument is just as self-deceptive a lie as 'money doesn't make you happy,' with which many excuse their laziness or their irresponsible attitude towards their finances. We owe it to each other to pay attention to our appearance, to take care of our cleanliness and to demand high standards of ourselves. These aren't simply things we do to make our life partner fall in love with us and commit to us before letting go of ourselves and doing what we would like to. We don't have to compete with the colleagues of our partner, who are twenty years younger, happy, and always pretty – rather, we should make our partner proud of us, happy for us, happy to look at us. With this, we can do a lot to ensure that our attention does not wander elsewhere, but keep our gaze where it needs to be. Plus, we're going to feel better.

In summary, I can emphasise the same thing I said about communication. If we can be kind to strangers, let us give our kindest words to the people who are most important to us. If we shave, get dressed, and comb our hair for the sake of others, how much more important it is to do the same for those who mean the most to us! They should get the best, the most beautiful, the sexiest of us!

Those who mean the most to us ... should get the best, the most beautiful, the sexiest of us!

When control falls out of our hands

There are quite extreme situations where people lose control of their own lives – such as an incapacitating addiction that initially seems to offset the difficulties of life, but then itself becomes the greatest difficulty that overgrows all other problems. The similarity between fighting addictions and storm-proof love is that order and personal hygiene are basic requirements for both. When something uncontrollable happens to us, taking back control of those things we have power over can give us a lot of strength. We talked about this and other practical aspects of the topic with Gábor Horváth, the director of Hope Rehabilitation House in Nágocs, Hungary.

What help can you give to people who have different addictions?

'We offer a half-a-year-long intensive group therapy programme where our days are organised down to the minute from half-past seven in the morning to half-past ten at night. We start and end each day with a joint evaluation, and in-between we learn with the patients together about how their illness works and discover the breaking points of their life, the emotional disturbances they couldn't process. In addition to these, we also analyse where they come from, what dysfunctions they bring from their families of origin, how they have repeated these, and how they might have passed these on.

'It is extremely important for us to be a community of companions in distress. "Older" patients who have been in the house for a longer time pass on their experiences and insights to those who come later, who ask questions and give feedback. Those who want to get sober and change can fight together for a common goal and go much further than during their previous solo attempts.

'Change always comes with pain, but anyone who takes on the "growth pains" ... usually leaves with a new foundation for life.'

'We also give many individual assignments, which will result in several hundred pages during a single therapy cycle. Change always comes with pain, but anyone who takes on the "growth pains" and doesn't quit the programme usually leaves with a new foundation for life.'

What influence do personal hygiene, an agenda, and an orderly living space have on recovery?

'In a word: huge! We work with a wide variety of addictions and have clearly found that the actual addiction is just a symptom of the problem. It doesn't matter if the problem is substance abuse (for example, alcohol, drugs, medication), behavioural addiction (video

games, screen addiction, workaholism, compulsive eating, or other eating disorders) or relationship addictions (companion addiction, co-dependence, sex and love addiction) – the lives of those who come to us are in ruins, so both their physical condition and their mental status need support, as well as the quality of their relationships. Many suffer from sleep disorders, depression and anxiety, and must live their lives with strong emotional fluctuations. We build from the bottom up in the programme: first we try to satisfy the basic needs and thereby stabilise the adhesion processes. It's part of the agenda that at half-past ten every day the light goes off in the house, abundant and healthy foods are served every day at the same time, a minimum of forty minutes' walk must be completed every day, the living space must always be kept tidy, and weekly sports are conducted, so this agenda unobtrusively but clearly stabilises and recharges the patients, providing a foundation on which they can build.'

'The lives of those who come to us are in ruins, so both their physical condition and their mental status need support.'

How can multi-year-old, maybe even decades-old habits be overwritten? For example, if someone has grown up in a messy home, has the opportunity to change slipped out of their grip?

'Creating and permanently incorporating a new habit is not an easy process; therefore we need to be able to spend at least six months together. At the beginning of every change, it is important to deal with resistance and pain. In the first months, it is often necessary to explain and confirm why it is important to practise and take the given steps – this is also a kind of helping control on our part. If all goes well, they get into the second stage relatively quickly, in a couple of weeks, by which time they already feel and experience the joys of change and the need to continue with those steps. It is quite easy to regress from this state. However, habits regularly exercised can become internal. By then, I'm already doing the good thing because it's my inner "programme",

and I miss it if I don't do it in my everyday life. In my view, every change has three basic conditions: my unhealthy conduct must hurt so much that I want to change it; then I must dare to ask for and accept help; and finally I must accept the "price" of change, which includes struggles, pain and temporary disruption.'

What effect does the process have on the marriages and family relationships of those involved?

'It has often been said in professional circles that addiction is a family illness. Unfortunately, most of those who come to us have really broken or damaged relationships. During therapeutic processes, we also examine where the blockages within the relationship are, and if there is co-dependence which is usually present. It can also be observed very often that addiction appears as a kind of painkiller or pleasure supplement in the already deformed relationship system, as a faulty coping mechanism. This is exactly why we have created a special group for family members, where they can also get help in recognising their own roles and injuries.

> **'It has often been said in professional circles that addiction is a family illness.'**

'If both parties are open to working with those who try to help them, each seeking their own responsibilities and not blaming each other as a scapegoat, there is a good chance that the relationship will be put on a new footing.'

What advice would you give to a husband who wants to change but has a hard time getting his partner to change?

'I often come across the question of what to do so that the other doesn't drink, doesn't work himself to death, doesn't spend money compulsively, doesn't look at pornographic sites, or doesn't stare at the screen with glassy eyes. My short answer is, "Nothing!" Because this is the wrong question. It is wrong because I want to change the other person; I will be the judge; I will make him responsible for the malfunctioning; and I will cease to be the partner who stands by him,

but I will either take on the role of a critical "parent" or a subordinate "child" who drifts with events.

'The right and important question is: "What can I do; how can I change; what is my role and responsibility? I really like the prayer I learnt from the co-dependent self-help groups. It goes, "God, give me peace of mind to accept people I can't change, courage to change who I can, and the wisdom to recognise: that person is me!" '

What is your message to couples who want to build a storm-proof relationship?

'I am convinced that the basis of a storm-proof relationship is, firstly, the stable personality. Awareness of my goals, priorities and tools is extremely important to be able to relate to the other family members in a healthy way. This, of course, doesn't mean that in difficult times my partner doesn't have to stand by me and maybe hold my hand, or that I don't have to hold his or hers. However, the foundation of my stability cannot be based on the current state of the other person, because if s/he falls, I will fall with him or her, too. There will be times when my partner and I won't stand on the same platform, when we must face the challenges that cause feelings of loneliness even at each other's side. At such times, having a source of strength from above is hugely important. Can I draw strength from God, who can calm even the storm? Can I receive guidance and support from Him? Can I fill my love tank so I am able to love my partner again?

'It is a basic necessity to have a ring-fenced time for just the two of us.'

'Thirdly, I consider it very important to pay attention to each other, especially in those life cycles where the stress of external challenges is greater. Such a period could be, for example, the arrival or growing up of children; the struggles and challenges of adolescence; or when we still take care of our children, but our parents already need our support. It is a basic necessity to have a ring-fenced time for just the two of us to be together and enjoy each other's company.'

STORM-PROOF LOVE

[82] Brianna Johnson et al., 'An Examination of Parent-Child Relationships and Teen Substance Use: A Brief Report', in: *Journal of Child & Adolescent Substance Abuse*, 2014/23, pp. 210-216; compare: *https://thefamilydinnerproject.org/about-us/benefits-of-family-dinners* (accessed: 14/08/2020)

[83] Stephen R. Covey, *The 7 Habits of Highly Effective People* (New York: Simon and Schuster, 1989), Kindle edition

[84] Birgitta Gatersleben, Isabelle Griffin, 'Environmental Stress', in: Ghozlane Fleury-Bahi, Enric Pol, Oscar Navarro (eds.), *Handbook of Environmental Psychology and Quality of Life Research* (Springer, 2017), pp. 469-486

[85] Quoted by: Darby E. Saxbe, Rena Repetti, 'No Place Like Home: Home Tours Correlate With Daily Patterns of Mood and Cortisol', in: *Personality and Social Psychology Bulletin*, 2010/36, pp. 71-81

[86] Alicia H. Clark, *Hack Your Anxiety: How to Make Anxiety Work for You in Life, Love, and All that You Do* (Naperville: Sourcebooks, 2018)

[87] Saustin Sampson Mfune, *Say NO to Drugs* (Nampa: Pacific Press, 2016)

[88] Rüdiger Hinsch, Ulrich Pfingsten, *Gruppentraining sozialer Kompetenzen, GSK* (Weinheim: Psychologie Verlags Union, 1998), p. 22

[89] Nancy Etcoff, *Survival of the Prettiest: The Science of Beauty* (New York: Anchor Books, 2000), p. 6

[90] I wrote in detail about crossing boundaries and how to protect your borders in this volume: *No More Games: How to Build a Faithful and Satisfying Relationship* (Alma Park, Grantham: Autumn House, 2018).

[91] Zachary Zeigler et al., 'Self-quarantine and weight gain related risk factors during the COVID-19 pandemic', in: *Obesity Research & Clinical Practice*, 2020/14, pp. 210-216

[92] Compare: Deborah Carr et al., 'Bigger Is Not Always Better: The Effect of Obesity on Sexual Satisfaction and Behaviour of Adult Men in the United States', in: *Men and Masculinities* 2013/16 (4), pp. 452-477, source: *https://doi.org/10.1177/1097184X13502651* (accessed: 20/08/2020)

Exercises

'Our home' tour guide

Imagine that your home is a tourist attraction, and you are the tour guide. What words would you use to introduce your home to visitors? Write down the words that come to mind first!

Entrance:

Living room:

Kitchen:

Bathroom:

Bedroom:

Other rooms:

How satisfied are you with the tour? What would you change in your home to present it in more positive words and be proud of it? What help do you ask from your partner for this to happen?

Let's cook something delicious together!

You and your family decide to prepare the food together today. You open the fridge, and you find the following: sour cream, butter, arugula, sun-dried tomatoes, chicken breast (or tofu), feta cheese, cucumber, and eggs. In the pantry you also find rice, some onions, and sweet potatoes.

Together, create a two-course menu from the ingredients listed (you don't have to use everything, but no other ingredients except spices are available). Describe the recipe:

Give the food a name:

Me in ten years

If you bumped into yourself in ten years' time, what kind of person would you like to see in front of you? Write it down in as much detail as you can!

Appearance (physique, clothing, aura):

Work:

Hobbies:

Social life and relationships:

STORM-PROOF LOVE

For this to happen in ten years, what decisions do you have to make today?

_____

_____

_____

_____

_____

_____

_____

_____

_____

_____

What kind of support would you ask from your partner to make all this happen?

_____

_____

_____

_____

_____

_____

_____

_____

_____

Emotional Availability:
'Are You There When I Need You?'

I was five years old when I lived with my parents in Cologne, Germany. I had some good experiences during that period, but I didn't like the kindergarten at all. When my parents left me there in the morning, I curled up in a corner and cried there alone until they came at noon to pick me up. I didn't eat, I didn't drink, and I didn't make friends either. My parents were puzzled. In the end, they made a difficult decision. Because the doctor said I needed change, they brought me home to my grandparents for a year to go to kindergarten there. I loved my grandparents very much; I loved kindergarten; and I went to the same preschool group as my cousin, who was also my best friend. However, something was wrong. Seemingly I blossomed, but I missed my parents terribly. Although I couldn't put it into words back then, an important basic belief deep inside me crumbled – that my parents would always be there for me, that they would always be available to me, and that I could always count on them.

> I loved my grandparents very much; I loved kindergarten.... However, something was wrong.

I have discussed this situation with my parents a hundred times. Although they loved me and tried to make the best possible decision at the time, the experience of being left alone caused me not to rely on others, not to depend on others, to want to solve everything by myself. I'm sure, as a parent, that I've made decisions myself that I later regretted. I always did my best – but, as the years went by, my best got better.[93]

We are beings created for attachment! We need the closeness, touch, and comfort of other people. As early as the 1700s, it was observed in orphanages that children whose basic physical needs were met but whose equally deep need for attachment was not met 'died in gloom'. Children left in the hospital in the 1940s were found to be in a state of 'debilitating mourning'.[94] The thesis that children need to touch a loving person, that they need a secure emotional attachment, has become generally accepted. For a long time, however, it was believed that grown-ups grow out of this emotional dependence by adulthood. The person who is dependent on others as an adult, who needs protection, closeness and love, has been branded for a long time, even in psychology, as weak, immature, co-dependent, undifferentiated, symbiotic, and so on.

'We now know that love is, in actuality ... the most compelling survival mechanism of the human species.'

The paradigm shift was brought about by a psychologist, John Bowlby, who extended attachment theory to the adult world as well. Contrary to the earlier position, 'Bowlby talked about "effective dependency", and how being able to turn to others for emotional support "from the cradle to the grave" is a sign and source of strength.'[95] This idea was further developed by Sue Johnson and completely rewrote everything we had thought about love so far: 'We now know that love is, in actuality ... the most compelling survival mechanism of the human species.' This is not because it induces us to mate and reproduce. We do manage to mate without love! Rather, it's because love drives us to bond emotionally with a few precious others who offer us a safe haven from the storms of life. 'Love is our bulwark, designed to provide emotional protection so we can cope with the ups and downs of existence. This drive to emotionally attach — to find someone to whom we can turn and say, "Hold me tight" – is wired into our genes and our bodies. It is as basic to life, health, and happiness as the drives for food, shelter, or sex.'[96]

We know very well by now that secure attachment also has a very positive effect on our individual functioning, so by no means can the claim be supported that whoever needs another person would be dependent or undifferentiated. We can best ask for and provide emotional support when we are emotionally safe ourselves. Besides, if we are securely attached to someone, it is easier for us to deal with the hurt they caused, and in a conflict situation we are less likely to become hostile or aggressive. People who are securely attached to another

person are more able to accept themselves. They are better able to rely on their own abilities; they have more confidence in resolving the tasks they face in life. They approach unknown situations more curiously, openly and creatively, and are more likely to achieve their goals.

What constitutes our emotional security and our secure attachment? Sue Johnson lists three qualities as the building blocks of emotional responsiveness:

1. **Accessibility** – that is, basic openness to a partner, even under pressure, uncertainty, or crisis. This openness means that our own emotions are also available to us, and we have the courage to face and engage them. The main question is, 'Can I reach you?'

2. **Responsiveness** – how we react to each other. What happens to the other also touches us, and we express it. We tune in to our partner and let him understand that his emotions, attachment needs, and fears affect us; they are important to us. The main question is, 'Can I rely on you to respond and care about my feelings?'

3. **Engagement** – that is, we do not listen to our partner's narrative as neutral listeners, but we stand by, support, and engage. Her story is our story, too; his pain is our pain, too. We also express this with respect in words and touch. The main question is, 'Will you value me, put me first, and stay close to me?'

'Can I rely on you to ... care about my feelings?'

The initials of the words form the acronym 'ARE', which is continued in emotionally focused therapy as: 'Are you there for me?' – meaning, 'Are you *here*; are you present to me?' This is exactly the essence of emotional reach: 'Are you here when I need you?' 'Can I count on you?' 'Can I reach you if there's a problem?' 'Does the thing that touches me move you too?' All this deeply determines the atmosphere of the relationship; it is also one of its most important quality indicators. 'Indeed, the lack of emotional responsiveness rather than the level of conflict is the best predictor of how solid a marriage will be five years into it. The demise of marriages begins with a growing absence of responsive intimate interactions. The conflict comes later.'[97]

STORM-PROOF LOVE

Let's see if this connection can be seen in action in the responses of the couples participating in our research![98]

	Statement	Developing couples	Declining couples
Accessibility	I can get my partner's attention easily.	88%	52%
	My partner is easy to connect with emotionally.	86%	44%
	My partner shows me that I come first with him/her.	86%	40%
	I am not feeling lonely or shut out in this relationship.	87%	44%
	I can share my deepest feelings with my partner. He/she will listen.	92%	50%

	Statement	Developing couples	Declining couples
Responsiveness	If I need connection and comfort, he/she will be there for me.	89%	43%
	My partner responds to signals that I need him/her to come close.	88%	44%
	I find I can lean on my partner when I am anxious or insecure.	88%	45%
	Even when we fight or disagree, I know that I am important to my partner and we will find a way to come together.	91%	59%
	If I need reassurance about how important I am to my partner, I can get it.	88%	47%

Statement		Developing couples	Declining couples
Engagement	I feel very comfortable being close to my partner, trusting my partner.	94%	62%
	I can confide in my partner about almost anything.	93%	58%
	I feel confident, even when we are apart, that we are connected to each other.	95%	61%
	I know that my partner cares about my joys, hurts, and fears.	90%	49%
	I feel safe enough to take emotional risks with my partner.	76%	37%

In all questions, a significant difference emerges between respondents in developing and declining relationships. Some questions were answered positively by double the number of respondents in a developing relationship, compared with respondents to the same questions who were in a declining relationship. It is also interesting to observe what the gender distribution shows. In short it can be stated, with a few exceptions, that women show 3-8% lower values than men. In other words, women feel less emotionally secure in a relationship than men. And this is indeed information to be taken very seriously, especially in light of the fact that women's greatest need in a relationship is emotional security.[99] Men, we need to change radically in this area! Because, in many families, men still earn more, many of us feel – I deliberately put it this way, because I am no exception – that we have done our part by providing financial security, and we can now sit back and feel comfortable. Financial security is an important component of making a marriage work (as we saw earlier), yet most couples who come to me for therapy are characterised by having enough money, yet not having a well-working relationship. It seems that, in addition to financial well-being, something else is needed for the success of our marriage.

Emotional availability is what the relationship feeds on. The experiential belief that we are important to each other, that our partner is standing by us and supports us in trouble, is the best reinforcement of the couple's 'we' consciousness. In Gottman's words, 'In the strongest marriages, husband and wife share a deep sense of meaning. They don't just "get along" – they also support each other's hopes and aspirations and build a sense of purpose into their lives together.'[100]

> 'In the strongest marriages, husband and wife share a deep sense of meaning. They don't just "get along" – they also support each other's hopes and aspirations.'

More than once I have experienced that in a difficult situation my wife, even in front of the whole world, closes ranks with me, assures me of her support, and is available to me. With this experience, I didn't have a hard time asking for help in the middle of the lockdown when I felt my mental balance waning. I had been preparing for months to climb Machu Picchu; I trained on the treadmill all winter; and then, when I got tired, I just closed my eyes and imagined the ancient structures in front of me . . . and now I was sitting there in my study, forced to give up one of my greatest passions and resources: travel. I was angry, tired, and frustrated. I felt my thinking narrowing more and more, which initially manifested itself only in silent grumbling, but then in a more and more audible discontent that could be heard from my words. I felt it would be unfair to my family not to let them know what was wrong with me, so I called Dóra and my daughter, Bogi, and told them, 'I feel like I'm not OK inside right now. I've become a bit tired of this whole situation. I'm under constant pressure to produce broadcasts, and I'm empty, I'm worried about my dad fighting cancer right in the middle of a pandemic, and I'm very angry that this virus has taken away from me what I've been waiting for for so long. Please be patient with me for now. If I speak to you a little more sharply, it is because of my inner tension and not because there is something wrong with you. I love you very much, but I'm not well inside now.'

The aftermath of this confession was shocking to me. My wife and daughter immediately took action to make me understand how important I was to them. My son called me more often just to enquire about my whereabouts. Dóra hugged me several times during the day so I could feel her care, and she cooked my favourite foods. Bogi called over her friend, with whom she arranged a board game party for me to make me feel better. I needed confirmation: 'Are you there for me? Can I count on you in trouble? Are you available to me when I need you?' And they clearly answered, 'Yes!'

[93] I like this expression so much that I borrowed it from Henry Cloud et al., *Unlocking Your Family Patterns* (Chicago, IL: Moody Publishers, 2011).
[94] See in detail in: Johnson, *Hold Me Tight!* Kindle edition.
[95] Ibid.
[96] Ibid.
[97] Ibid.
[98] Questions taken from: Sue Johnson, Kenneth Sanderfer, *Created for Connection: The 'Hold Me Tight' Guide for Christian Couples* (New York, Boston, London: Little, Brown and Company), pp. 68-69
[99] According to John Gottman's research, the most common relationship-oriented complaints of women are: 'He is never there for me' and 'There isn't enough intimacy and connection.' See John Gottman, Julie Schwartz Gottman, *The Man's Guide to Women* (New York: Rodale, 2016), p. 6.
[100] John M. Gottman, Nan Silver, *The Seven Principles of Making Marriage Work*, Kindle edition

STORM-PROOF LOVE

Exercise

The following questions will help you to assess how emotionally available you are to each other. I suggest that you first answer the questions on your own, and then talk about the answers with each other, too.

1. The biblical creation story says of Adam and Eve that 'they were both naked, the man and his wife, and were not ashamed.'[101] On a scale of 1 to 10, how brave are you to emotionally strip yourself in front of your partner? What is the reason for this?

2. What past or present events are preventing you from taking on greater vulnerability and opening up emotionally to your partner?

3. What negative experiences have you had regarding emotional disclosure, either in your relationship or as part of your relationship with your parents or other important people (for example, did you trust someone who later abused that trust)?

4. What positive experiences do you have with emotional revelation?

_____

_____

_____

_____

5. In what situations did you feel best when your partner stood by you?

_____

_____

_____

_____

6. What do you ask your partner to do in order for you to risk opening up more easily and making yourself vulnerable to him/her?

_____

_____

_____

_____

7. What can you do to make your partner more trusting in you?

_____

_____

_____

_____

[101] Genesis 2:25

STORM-PROOF LOVE

Spirituality
– the Engine Room of the Relationship

By now, you probably know by heart one of the recurring theses of this book: the crisis shows how many reserves we have. The following biblical story is about this principle.

A desperate father asked Jesus' disciples to help his son, whose mysterious illness no one had been able to heal. The attempts of the disciples themselves had been in vain, but Jesus, seeing the father's despair, healed the boy.

Both the crowd and the disciples were puzzled by the disciples' failure to heal the boy. To their questions, Jesus answered, 'Howbeit this kind goeth not out but by prayer and fasting.'[102] This finding is interesting, because we do not read that Jesus prayed or fasted in connection with the healing. It would have been strange if He had started fasting, because, according to longstanding religious practice, fasting usually takes at least a day. The only reasonable explanation is that Jesus did not pray and fast then, but was able to heal the boy by using His prayer and fasting reserves from before. He did not build up His reserves in the crisis. This story also confirms our motto: the storm shows how many reserves we have – even in a spiritual sense.

He did not build up his reserves in the crisis. This story also confirms our motto: the storm shows how many reserves we have.

In this chapter, we examine this important dimension of human existence, the upward dimension, and examine the impact of spirituality on the storm resistance of our relationship.

'There are no atheists on a sinking ship'

According to the old saying, 'There are no atheists on a sinking ship.' The pandemic seems to partly justify this thesis. During the first wave of the coronavirus, I observed three types of attitudes towards spirituality. There were couples whose faith and its common practice had been an integral part of their lives before. These couples had a special reserve, had something to fall back on in the crisis, and their faith provided them with a stronghold of hope and encouragement. They are the ones whom Gábor Horváth mentioned in our conversation as those who in the storm were able to cling to the God who can calm the storm.

Others had cultivated a more distant relationship with faith, but in trouble they remembered where to look to. Once the storm is over, most of them will be overwhelmed with daily tasks again, and faith will be pushed out of their lives again.

> There were couples whose faith and its common practice had been an integral part of their lives before. These couples had a special reserve, had something to fall back on in the crisis, and their faith provided them with a stronghold of hope and encouragement.

Finally, there are people who consciously deny all contact with the supernatural, faith or spirituality, especially in its institutionalised, organised forms. At the same time, they are still looking for something to hold onto that could be the centre of their lives. They would not put it that way, but this would play a role similar to that of a deity. For them this could be a political idea, an esoteric practice, or just universal scepticism.

At the beginning of the book, on the topic of emotional health, I stated: an emotionally healthy person knows what the focus of his life should be, and what should be in the margin. This is also of great importance in the area of spirituality. What is in the middle of our lives, and what is on the edges? Man is a being seeking the supernatural, open to the supernatural. Therefore, there is nothing unusual about looking upward instinctively in troubled times. This is like following a built-in programme, seeking answers, help and strength. This was also observed during lockdown. When churches and congregations closed, the views of online worship reached an unprecedented peak. Online events that were previously watched by only a few dozen people have now frequently got thousands or even tens of thousands of views.

STORM-PROOF LOVE

People were clearly open to faith, because they saw that control over events was out of their hands, and they needed the assurance that amid all the trouble a higher force could keep things under control.

In the research, I examined issues related to living and practising faith and its compatibility between partners, rather than dogmatic theorems, so that, regardless of denomination, anyone could identify with the statements.

Statement	Developing couples	Declining couples
I am happy with the way we live out our faith.	64%	37%
We can rely on our faith in difficult times.	73%	50%
Our practised belief brings us closer together.	63%	23%
Differences in the values of our faith cause tension in our relationship.	6%	16%
For us, faith is a personal experience rather than a religious formality.	73%	49%

Here, too, the figures convincingly demonstrate that the studied area is an important component of relational resilience, and that it is also clear that couples who have shared beliefs – or who are 'spiritually compatible', in technical language – are more likely to have a positive trajectory than those who do not live according to any kind of faith, or whose faith is not lived out in harmony with each other's beliefs (in other words, they are spiritually incompatible). Depending on our personal attitude, faith can be a resource in a relationship, but it can also be a source of serious conflict. When faith is a personal resource for both parties, and they live their faith in harmony with each other, it becomes their common resource and brings them closer together.[103]

Not all beliefs are beneficial

We have already formulated an important thesis about faith and beliefs in the section on finance, and it is even more important in this topic: 'We have power over what we believe, but what we believe will have power over us.'

This sentence refutes the wisdom of my grandfather, who always closed our discourses on faith by saying, 'Son, it doesn't matter who believes what, so long as they take it seriously.' But it does matter! It is very

> 'We have power over what we believe, but what we believe will have power over us.'

important for us to understand what belief system, what principles, what teachings we have adopted, because they will have a tangible effect on every segment of our lives, and of course on the quality of our marriage. Many times, an extreme pattern of behaviour or some kind of mental disorder can be explained by beliefs that may have been imparted to us in good faith, but which then ended up having a very bad effect.

There's the old farmer who closed every marriage dispute by saying, 'Let the woman be silent.' After some research, it turns out that our man as a child had always heard from the priest that a man is much more valuable than a woman, because Eve picked the fruit from the forbidden tree. The woman is therefore subordinate to the man.

Or there's the man in his thirties with sexual dysfunction, whose marriage is suffering because of his premature ejaculation. During our conversations, he recounted how deeply he was influenced as a teenager by his parents' rhetoric about moral purity and the damning effects of sexual sins. He recalled his struggles, how he cried while masturbating, and then feared that he would go to hell. Is it any wonder that the command forbidding sexuality is so deeply ingrained in his soul that his body is trying to quickly overcome this terrible sin?

Finally, I can mention the young man who responded to my question about faith with an aggressive expression, saying only: 'We shall leave this topic alone. I grew up in religious terror.'

Not all beliefs are good. There are those that build, bless, and heal, but there are also those that cripple, oppress, and cause illness. I know there are many approaches to faith, but since I myself, like most people in this part of the world, am rooted in and identify with Christianity, allow me to draw my examples from here.

I often come across wedding invitations with the following biblical quotation: 'Two people are better than one, because they can reap more benefit from their labor. For if they fall, one will help his companion up, but pity the person who falls down and has no one to help him up. Furthermore, if two lie down together, they can keep each other warm, but how can one person keep warm by himself? Although an assailant may overpower one person, two can withstand him. Moreover, a three-stranded cord is not quickly broken.'[104] I've always liked the list of why the two people are better together than alone, but for a long time I didn't know what to do with the last sentence. How does the 'triple thread' come into a relationship? Then I understood: the third thread is God's mysterious presence in marriage. He is the only third person who does not endanger the integrity of the marriage, but makes it stronger.

This image became even more meaningful to me as I began to explore in studies how the tensile strength of a rope changes when braided from multiple strands. I have found that if two ropes with a tensile strength of fifty pounds each are braided together, their tensile strength will add up, so the new rope will already be able to withstand a hundred pounds. However, adding a third thread will increase the load capacity not just by fifty pounds, but by doubling the joint tensile strength of the previous two strands, meaning such a rope can withstand two hundred pounds! And this is exactly what our research has shed light on. God's presence in the relationship doubles its tensile strength.

> **God's presence in the relationship doubles its tensile strength.**

Of course, all this only happens if faith is a personal experience, an integral part of life, not just an empty ritual. The study also confirms this: 73% of respondents living in a developing relationship were able to identify with this statement, while only half of those living in a less resilient relationship were able to say the same.

With this chapter, I would like to encourage you, as the only person who has the right to do so, to ask yourself the following questions: does my faith influence my life in the right direction? Do my beliefs make me happier? When I think of God, does a feeling of love and respect appear in me, or rather fear and compulsion to conform? Does my faith make me a better husband, father, wife, or mother? Believe well to live well!

Does my faith make me a better husband, father, wife, or mother? Believe well to live well!

Esoteria is not a friend of marriage

I am afraid this statement has made many people feel uncomfortable; but, unfortunately, I have come to this conclusion from my personal experiences. Esoteria is trying to satisfy a real need in a very dangerous way. It exploits the general human desire for the supernatural, which in many cases is not satisfied by institutionalised and impersonal ecclesiastical religiosity.

Spirituality originally meant a faith lived out in practice, yet more and more people today identify the term with esoteric practices. What makes them dangerous for marriage is precisely the fact that their conclusions are not based on observation, objective factors, or scientific research, but on internal intuitions, which are always under the influence of the momentary mood. Based on these, people make decisions that determine the lives of entire families for decades. I can cite many tragic examples of this that I remember from my counselling practice.

Tamara came to couple's therapy to clear herself of her husband's accusations that she had an affair with her co-worker. Anton believed in his wife's guilt with full conviction; but, as evidence, he listed arguments that would puzzle any sober-minded person. He phoned in to tarot card readers who practise on TV; and, independently, fortune-tellers told him that his wife had been having an extramarital

STORM-PROOF LOVE

affair. Tamara was in a real state of shock: firstly, because her husband accused her, even though she had never flirted with other men even for a second; secondly, because, after many phone calls, her husband received a six-digit phone bill. All this came despite the fact that Anton was not a stupid man: he was a university graduate working in a responsible position. Their marriage couldn't bear this. They got divorced.

Annamaria was looking for help in solving her sleep problems when her mother invited her to a 'lecture'. At the event, a man in his sixties talked about how to put the energy of angels at the service of healing, and then gave a very impressive presentation. The young mother of three then began to go for 'treatments' on a regular basis, during which he passed on the energy of the angels to the woman through a 'healing' touch, while also touching her intimate body parts. After a few 'treatments', the man announced that he could only cure particularly stubborn sleep disorders through internal treatment, which meant they had to have sex – of course, solely for the noble purpose of healing. The young woman is now struggling with the issue of whether to tell her husband what happened, or to keep the secret to herself. She feels dirty, exploited, and deceived — and she still can't sleep, just like before! Her torments are only multiplied by the realisation that the healer has given her mother the same 'treatment'.

> **The young woman is now struggling with the issue of whether to tell her husband what happened, or to keep the secret to herself.**

Monica was a teacher who felt burned out after twenty years of teaching, and was looking to learn a new profession. In her search she came across a female self-help club which promised to help her find her inner voice, showing her a sure direction in an uncertain phase of life. Thanks to the group's participation, she increasingly 'heard' this voice, which told her to leave her family as they were holding back her spiritual development. She wanted to talk about this with her husband, but her new friends advised her against it. She was told that she could only be true to herself if she followed the inner voice without allowing herself to be distracted from her own path. Since the family did not have the opportunity to have a say in Monica's decision, a baffled husband and two teenagers at a very sensitive age are now grieving over the ruins of a broken family.

The list could go on and on. When we are disappointed in our partner, the 'inner voice' – that is, our momentary emotional state – makes us do very selfish things. If we were to follow all such urges in the name of self-identity, we would do a great deal of harm to those around us. However, what is needed in a storm is to treat momentary emotions carefully and with caution, and rather to listen to our decisions. Our motto in a storm should be, 'I do not do what *feels* right, but what *is* right.'

Emotionally healthy spirituality

As we have seen, in the field of spirituality, it *does* matter what direction we take, so we cannot escape the seemingly difficult but very rewarding process of information gathering, reflection, decision-making, and lifelong self-discovery. Within Christian spirituality, we find very liberated, happy, and life-affirming people; and, unfortunately, we also find those tormented by guilt, uncertain of God's acceptance and love, and radiating uncertainty and bitterness towards others. The difference between the two attitudes is emotional health. Although the subject has been known for a long time, a systematic processing of the topic did not begin until the 2000s. One of the pioneers of this work is Peter Scazzero, whose books have become bestsellers.

> 'It is impossible for a Christian to be spiritually mature while remaining emotionally immature.'

According to Scazzero, 'It is impossible for a Christian to be spiritually mature while remaining emotionally immature.' He then goes on to say, 'For some reason, however, the vast majority of Christians today live as if the two concepts have no intersection. Our standards of what it means to be "spiritual" totally bypass many glaring inconsistences. We have learnt to accept that:

- You can be a dynamic, gifted speaker for God in public while being an unloving spouse and parent at home.
- You can function as a church board member or pastor while being unteachable, insecure, and defensive.
- You can memorise entire books of the New Testament while still being unaware of your depression and anger, even displacing it on other people.
- You can fast and pray a half-day a week for years as a spiritual discipline while constantly being critical of others, justifying it as "discernment".
- You can lead hundreds of people in a Christian ministry while being driven by a deep personal need to compensate for a nagging sense of failure.
- You can pray for deliverance from the demonic realm when in reality you are simply avoiding conflict, repeating an unhealthy pattern of behaviour traced back to the home in which you grew up.
- You can be outwardly cooperative at church while unconsciously trying to undercut or defeat your supervisor by coming habitually late, constantly forgetting meetings, withdrawing and becoming apathetic, or ignoring the real issue behind why you are hurt and angry.'[105]

I couldn't recover from the shock for days after I first read these thoughts. I am not used to having someone speak so openly in a Christian context about the importance of emotional health. On the other hand, I have come across many instances where Christians suppress their emotions, branding them as bad, devilish, or sinful . . . and condemning the feelings of others is a sure way to spiritually and emotionally cripple the members of the community.

> **I couldn't recover from the shock for days after I first read these thoughts. I am not used to having someone speak so openly.**

Scazzero accuses Christianity that it has arbitrarily exiled emotions from the complex reality of human existence – consisting of emotional, social, intellectual, spiritual, and physical dimensions – and placed a disproportionate emphasis on the intellectual and spiritual dimensions. This necessarily leads to imbalance. The solution is to learn to reconnect to our emotions, recognise them, understand their message, and learn to control them as well.

This is something essential to spiritual welfare as well, as 'God speaks to us through a knot in the stomach, muscle tension, trembling and shaking, the release of adrenaline into our bloodstream, headaches, and a suddenly elevated heart rate. God may be screaming at us through our physical body while we look for (and prefer) a more "spiritual" signal. The reality is that often our bodies know our feelings before our minds.'[106]

> **The solution is to learn to reconnect to our emotions, recognise them, understand their message, and learn to control them as well.**

Scazzero defines emotionally healthy spirituality in six stages:

1. Look beneath the surface

An emotionally healthy person sees herself and the other person as an iceberg, an essential part of whom is hidden deep beneath the surface. Such a person has learnt to pay attention to the heart, to relate to her inner feelings, and to what is happening in her inner world. She deals with the reasons, the deeper motives behind her actions.

2. Break the power of the past

An important component of an emotionally healthy spirituality is facing the personal and family past. In this process, the person identifies the legacy of values and behaviours he has inherited from previous generations, and draws a conclusion of what he wants to keep and what he wants to replace with new ways of coping.

STORM-PROOF LOVE

3. Live in brokenness and vulnerability

The Bible is full of imperfect characters. Moses stuttered and killed a man; Hosea had a prostitute as his wife; Jonah fled from God; Martha was too worried; Noah got drunk ... and we could list many more! The mature person takes ownership of his imperfections and does not hide them ... and, as he says yes to himself, just as God says yes to him, he embarks on the path of healing and change.

> The mature person takes ownership of his imperfections and does not hide them ... and, as he says yes to himself, just as God says yes to him, he embarks on the path of healing and change.

4. Receive the gift of limits

Boundaries not only hinder, but also provide room for improvement where we can operate safely. The lack of boundaries does not result in perfect freedom, but in anxiety. If we accept our boundaries, we will no longer want to become the person God has never intended us to be, but we will embark on the path by which we can evolve into the best possible version of ourselves.

5. Embrace grieving and loss

Those who always flee from sorrow and loss do not process it, but box emotions in, or they suppress them in their souls and store them on the bottom shelf of the imaginary closet. This box becomes a ticking time bomb, poisoning the soul from within. However, facing and coping with negative emotions helps us become more compassionate people. In fact, we will only be able to identify with the suffering of others to the extent that we have allowed ourselves to experience our own losses.

6. Make the incarnation your model for loving well

The birth and incarnation of Jesus as a human being is the best example of love. By becoming human, He entered our world, but at the same time remained in His own world, because He remained God in forgiving sins, healing the sick and raising the dead. This is how He formed a bridge between the two worlds. These steps can also serve for us as a model of true love, so that we do not lose our own identity in the other person as we dare to enter their world, and neither are we left unmoved by what happens to the other person by remaining in our own world; rather, we build a bridge between the two worlds.

Lessons of the lockdown for religious communities

The crisis has shown how many reserves we had. This is true not only for the individual and the family, but also for religious communities. The time of the pandemic made it clear which communities were in connection with their surroundings and understood the language and life situation of those whom they served, and which were the communities living a hermit existence locked up in their own separate time and space. Many realised the need for agents of hope in a situation full of fear and uncertainty. They armed themselves and began to proclaim messages of hope to contemporary people in a contemporary way. These communities and individual initiatives became the centre of attention incredibly quickly, and the previous few-dozen views on their social media channels jumped to thousands, or sometimes to tens of thousands. Then the doors of churches and congregations opened again, and it became apparent whether the communities themselves had learnt something from the pandemic. Many who hadn't had much to do with Christianity before made an attempt to visit a religious community. The lucky ones found an inclusive community with a good atmosphere; others left in frustration and returned to their old lives. In order that the retention ability of the church community might not only depend on luck, I have gathered some lessons for the future that I observed during COVID-19. The inclusive and retaining religious community must be:

> Many realised the need for agents of hope in a situation full of fear and uncertainty. They armed themselves and began to proclaim messages of hope.

STORM-PROOF LOVE

1. Flexible

Instead of the 'we've always done it this way' mentality, this community is open to change. It does not force the same solution on all situations, but selects the solution that best suits the present challenge from a broader repertoire of solutions. It is able to think outside of the box, and does not stifle creativity, but supports it.

2. Age- and culture-sensitive

Such a religious community lives with the people it attempts to reach. Its members know and speak their language (instead of an internal jargon), know what their challenges are, and give practical answers to them. This community is not afraid of questions, but welcomes them as opportunities for dialogue. Its furnishings are contemporary, modern, and don't feel like a museum. The members of the community are contemporary people, and this is reflected in their attire as well – not some weird monks, stuck here from the past. It uses technical tools boldly and consciously, updates its website regularly, and is active and aware on social media platforms. We need to acknowledge that whoever does not have a relevant message during a crisis will not have an audience after the crisis!

> A good community life can counterbalance a mediocre sermon; but no brilliant preaching can offset the effects of a bad community.

3. Community-centred

The inclusive religious community is not performance-oriented, where the success or failure of worship depends on a single person or a narrow group, but it is community-oriented. It is not an audience, but a community. In the 1990s, conversions were tied to the ministry of a high-impact preacher. Many communities are stuck in this approach and wonder why there is no growth. Today, conversions occur in communities under the influence of authentic disciples. A good community life can counterbalance a mediocre sermon; but no brilliant preaching can offset the effects of a bad community. The measurements of a real community: how much time do members spend together outside the walls of the church? How much do they laugh together? How often do they eat together? Who will be contacted first if there is a problem? Are you waiting for the show, or meeting friends?

4. Friendly

Every community has a unique atmosphere, a 'feel'. As soon as someone enters, this atmosphere strikes the person, and the person makes a decision on whether he wants to come back again or not. There are communities with an atmosphere of love and respect, and there are those with an atmosphere of authority and fear. There are places where people go because of a sense of duty, but they would be ashamed in front of their friends to admit where they are going; and there are places people are happy to go to, and they invite everyone else to visit because it is so pleasant to be there.

> As soon as someone enters, this atmosphere strikes the person, and the person makes a decision on whether he wants to come back again or not.

5. Conscious

The conscious church has a mission statement, and knows why it exists, and all its members work together to achieve this common goal. This awareness informs the themes of worship, printed and online communication, the type of events organised. It does its own duty and has courage to let go of what someone else is doing. This community has a plan for where it wants to be in 5-10 years, and is currently working to make that plan a reality.

6. Growth-oriented

In addition to consciousness, growth is also an important value for the inclusive and retaining community, both individually and collectively. The community itself develops in an identifiable direction, but the community events also supply quality fuel to individual development. Participants are also driven by a desire for growth; and, if they look back on the past years, they can specifically name the areas where they have grown thanks to being members of the community. If they were to drop out, they would miss something important that is necessary to move forwards. It is not the hospice of the saints, but the training camp of the disciples!

This list may sound utopian, but high standards are very important to me, not only in my marriage and individual spiritual life, but also in my community life. I don't want to settle for anything less!

[102] Matthew 17:21

[103] I included non-religious and incompatible couples in the same group, because it has become clear from previous research that both cases have a similar effect on the relationship, as opposed to instances where the parties have a shared faith. The spiritually harmonious couples are producing significantly better results than the previous two groups, which are not significantly different from each other in their results. Compare: Larson and Olson, 'Spiritual Beliefs and Marriage: A National Survey Based on ENRICH'.

[104] Ecclesiastes 4:9-12, NET

[105] Peter Scazzero, The Emotionally Healthy Church (Grand Rapids: Zondervan, 2003), pp. 50, 51

[106] Peter Scazzero, Emotionally Healthy Spirituality (Grand Rapids: Zondervan, 2017), p. 46

Exercises

What do you tell your child?

Suppose your preschool child bombards you daily with countless questions. You cannot just simply answer anything to these questions. What would you answer to the questions that go beyond visible reality?

'In the kindergarten, Danny told me that they used to pray in the evenings. What does that mean and why do they do it?'

_____

_____

_____

_____

'Is it really true that humans evolved from a monkey?'

_____

_____

_____

'Suzy goes to church every weekend to worship. Why do people go there, and what do they do there?'

_____

_____

_____

_____

STORM-PROOF LOVE

'Where is Grandfather now? What does it mean that someone dies; what happens to him? Will we see him again?'

_____

_____

_____

'Why is Jesus such an important person that so many celebrate His birthday at Christmas?'

_____

_____

_____

'When you're not with me, am I completely alone? Who will take care of me then? And why can't I see God?'

_____

_____

_____

_____

Talk about faith!

The following questions can be good starters in which you can find out how each other feels and thinks about faith, what experiences you have had in this area. Ask each other a question from the list in alternating order. You may move line by line, but you can also choose any from the questions.

❊ What role did faith play in your family of origin?
❊ Was anyone particularly religious in your wider family, and what did the family think of this person?

❀ How did your family relate to religious holidays (Christmas, Easter, and so on)?

❀ What do you think about the origin of life?

❀ Why do you think we are in this world?

❀ Do good and bad exist in an absolute sense, or is it all just a matter of subjectivity?

❀ Do you think faith and science support or exclude each other?

❀ Which major world religion are you most sympathetic to, and why?

❀ Does it matter who chooses which religion?

❀ Is it allowed to change someone's faith?

❀ Have you ever had any supernatural experiences? If so, what change has this experience made in your life?

❀ Do you think God exists? If so, how do you envision Him?

❀ What will you ask God when you meet Him?

❀ Do you think faith can be harmful?

❀ What are the benefits of believing?

❀ What do you do if you're in trouble and can't find help?

❀ Have you ever prayed and then something changed?

❀ Do you think faith is an expression of weakness or strength?

❀ What was your most unpleasant experience with faith or religion?

❀ Is there something you admire in believing people; maybe you envy them for something?

❀ Who is the most authentic believer for you?

❀ Has anyone ever tried to convince you of their own beliefs? How did you feel then? What was your reaction?

❀ What role do you intend faith to play in our marriage or family life?

❀ What would our family gain from giving faith a greater role in our lives?

❀ What do you think we should represent to our children about faith?

❀ Do you want to change something in our lives in the area of spirituality? Do you think we should train ourselves in this area? What should we read or listen to?

❀ Would you like to pray with me?

STORM-PROOF LOVE

Training Plan for Storm-proof Love

The storm resistance of your love is not born in the storm. The storm only brings to the surface how many reserves you have accumulated. I have emphasised this principle many times throughout this book. If you are in a storm-free period now, this is the best time to train your relationship. If, on the other hand, the clouds are already gathering, it is time to take a deep breath and begin to translate the findings of our research into your everyday life with great commitment and discipline. In the second case, you are moving forwards on a slightly more difficult road, because we acquire new knowledge and customs more easily if we can afford to experiment and to make mistakes without consequences. Under pressure, we naturally tend to use long-confessed methods, whether they are useful or not. So, let's start doing a workout plan that you can practise during quiet periods so the storm will find you ready when it comes.

If you are in a storm-free period now, this is the best time to train your relationship.

I really like it when complex systems that seem complicated are presented with a metaphor or image that is easy to grasp. It makes them easier to store in our memory; and, with their help, longer lists or correlations that are more difficult to see at first glance can be recalled and easily applied in an emergency.

I was just sweating under the weights in the gym when I started to think about how I could express everything I'd discovered during the research visually in a memorable way. It should be so simple that we can print it out on a single sheet and hang it on the refrigerator door, so that the seven secrets of a happy and balanced relationship can be ingrained into us as we look at it every day. It was then that I saw a lady climbing endlessly on a step machine, and I realised that a staircase might be the proper symbol of the road to a storm-proof love. In the days that followed, I couldn't let go of this picture; it was constantly brewing in my mind. Finally, the following model, which can also be used as a training plan, was compiled, and it summarises well the most important insights we learnt from the participants in the research.

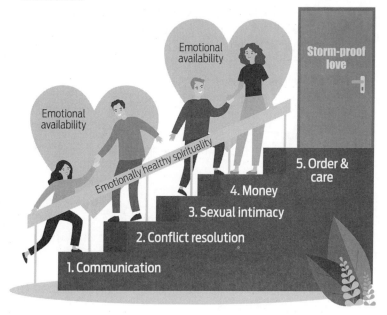

There are five steps leading to storm-proof love:

1. Communication
- Let's share our emotions!
- Keep the kindest and most beautiful words for the most important people!

If you remember the chapter on communication, you may remember, for example, the practice of being a sports commentator, or that vulgar expressions are not an expression of trust, but more like a woodworm that eats the structure of your love from the inside out until it collapses.

2. Conflict resolution
• Let's look calmly at the root of things!

As I presented in the chapter on conflict management, the main question is whether we are only dealing with the surface (the overboiling part of the soup), or whether we are talking about what the issue is really about. It is vital that all this happens in a kind and calm atmosphere, because if we let the tension prevail, we will get further and further away from a peaceful solution.

3. Sexual intimacy
• Stress-reducing response to deeper needs in the language of personal sex.

Now you also know that stress affects people's libido in different ways: it may increase sexual appetite for some, but can greatly reduce it for others. It's important for you to recognise that when you think you desire sex, you may really have desires on deeper levels as well, and you should start experimenting to have as many personal/synchronised sexual encounters with each other as possible.

4. Money
• Review your beliefs, savings, and decision-making together.

It turns out that money issues and worries about money have a lot to do with whether we feel good about our relationship or not.

It turns out that money issues and worries about money have a lot to do with whether we feel good about our relationship or not. Therefore, even before the storm, it is important to accumulate adequate reserves. And it is a great help to do this if we have beliefs that promote our material well-being, if we learn to manage our resources together and make joint decisions about money.

5. Order and care

- Smart home, smart appearance, and smart agenda.

We've learnt a proven method: if something happens to us over which we have no control, we can more easily deal with it if we begin to control what we have power over. Thus, the crisis had less severe effects on those couples who kept their homes tidy during lockdown, who were well-groomed even if they did not have to go to work, and who kept a disciplined agenda.

These five steps indicate specific tasks. There is no need for special prerequisites, and the exercises listed at the end of the chapters will help you to practise them. I note here that the order of the steps is not random. In order to develop our relationship, communication is the foundation. How would we be able to resolve our financial differences if we didn't have the basic skills to share our emotions, formulate our opinions, and listen to what our partner has to say? We can then turn our attention to how to resolve our disagreements and bring them to a common platform, which is conflict management. It is not worth going into a debate about our different notions of order until we have learnt to actively express our love and respect to each other, even when we have differing views. This is followed by sexuality, which, together with the previous two steps, belongs to the interpersonal inner world of the relationship. It contributes immensely to making you feel like a strong, unbreakable team, each other's allies; and, as allies, it's already much easier to deal with forces and factors that are beyond your control but still have a strong impact on you both. This is where money and order come into play.

In addition to the above five steps, there are two other factors that are important components of a storm-proof love. These are less about what you are doing, and more about what you are. That is why I did

> I note here that the order of the steps is not random. In order to develop our relationship, communication is the foundation.

not formulate them as steps, but as attitudes. This is because they strongly influence the way you communicate, the way you handle conflicts, the way you express affection, the way you relate to money, and the environment you create around you.

These two meta-factors are:

1. Emotional accessibility

It is a matter of attitude how accessible you are to each other in trouble. Are you convinced based on your past experiences that you are important to each other, that your pain, worries and fears touch each other, and that you can count on your partner's understanding and compassion? Of course, emphasising attitudes instead of actions does not mean that progress cannot be made in practical ways in these areas. This is because our attitude is made up of a series of our daily decisions and actions. So, if we start to open up to each other more consciously and pay more attention to supporting each other emotionally, we can experience very positive changes.

2. Spirituality

This is also a basic attitude: I would say that it is a summary of your basic attitudes towards life (faith is what we believe to be true; values are what we consider important; and our behaviour is a consequence of these two). The couple in the picture cling to it like a banister, just as we cling in the storm to the One who can calm the storm, and this experience also re-frames our life after the storm. However, the content and object of our faith does matter. Our faith is not something we received (or did not receive) a given measure of at birth, but rather is something we can develop and grow through gathering information, through conducting deep and honest conversations, and through self-reflection.

Faith is what we believe to be true; values are what we consider important; and our behaviour is a consequence of these two.

As I have tried to show you the building blocks of storm-proof love in more detail throughout the pages of this volume, I hope I have succeeded in convincing you that every relationship can change, grow, and develop – including yours! Whatever a crisis brings out of you is like a medical finding. It shows you where your strengths are, and what areas in your relationship need to be improved. I am confident that our research has given you not only theoretical information, but also knowledge that can be transformed into everyday practice in order to achieve a resilient, happy, storm-proof love relationship. What the many components of storm-proof love have in common is that you have control over each of them! If I have managed to convince you of this, it was worthwhile for me to conduct the research and write this book, and it was worthwhile for you to read it.

Warmest regards,

Dr Gábor Mihalec